The Freedom of Zen

The Zen book
that shatters all limits
and bounds

Translation © 2009 by John Kitching

Original title: "Die Freiheit des Zen"
Published by Schirner Verlag Darmstadt 2007

Producer and publisher: Books on Demand GmbH, Norderstedt

Cover motive: Zen-Patriarchs
Ink drawing by Zensho W. Kopp

Cover design by Michel Schmidt,
Jörg Zimmermann
Text setting by Torsten Zander

All rights reserved. This book, or parts thereof, may not be reproduced in any form without permission.

Visit our website at
http://www.zenmeditation.org/

ISBN: 978-3-83916-893-6

Contents

Preface 5
1. The Directness Of Zen 9
2. The Highest Truth Is Not Difficult 23
3. Stop Searching 33
4. When The Soap Bubble Bursts. 43
5. At The Moment Of Death 51
6. True Zen Practise. 61
7. There Is Nothing To Achieve 73
8. A Thunderclap In A Clear Blue Sky 93
9. See Things As They Are 105
10. Be Here Now! 117
11. The Eternal Tao 125
12. Love Is The All-Embracing Whole 135
13. No Zen Without Enlightenment. 143
14. The Original State Of The Mind. 157
15. The Everyday Mind Is The Way 167
16. Directly Grasping Reality. 177
Glossary 185
Contact 209

Preface

The talks published in this book, by one of the greatest spiritual masters of our times, contain the power to shock our ego at its foundations.

In "The Freedom of Zen", Zen Master Zensho shows us how we can free ourselves of the slavery of autonomous compulsive thinking, and how we can enter into the enlightened state of pure consciousness.

In a refreshing, contemporary way, Zensho teaches an entirely free Zen which is not attached to any particular form. With all means at his disposal, he endeavours to awaken us from the slumber of habitude; for habitude in whatever form it may be, prevents us from directly experiencing reality.

In the talks chosen here, the master shows us the mirror of our true being, and we recognise in it our buddha-nature; our original state of Enlightenment, which is constantly present.

Again and again he points to the fact that the truth cannot be expressed, and that it is beyond all words. For words are merely guideposts, just like the finger that points to the moon. But we must not stick to the finger with the false notion that it be the moon.

Zensho's humorous geniality and his unconventional, free way of teaching bestow a tremendous vitality and presence on his talks.

In a vivid and true-to-life way he imparts to us the path to liberation, and by means of many citations, lets the Zen Masters of old have their say. For example, a quote from one of the old masters is taken up and illuminated and unexpectedly, a comparison from everyday life comes to aid and elucidates the quote at hand.

In Zensho's talks we feel the realisation and freedom of one of the greatest awakened beings of our times. His arousing words of shocking openness are filled with such spiritual force that they can hit us like a bolt of lightening. And thus, it can often happen that the logic of our conceptual discriminating thought is smashed, so that we can comprehend the truth that lies beyond all words. Without compromise, everything is swept away such that we become able to reach the boundless freedom of the Mind.

By publishing these talks, we hope that this book will reach the hands of all those who are spiritually mature for the enlightened words of one of the greatest enlightened beings of our times.

These are words of inexhaustible profound wisdom which transform and liberate us. May this book help liberate all those who read it.

January 2007 　　　　　　　　　　　　　　The editors
Tao Chan Zen-Centre, Wiesbaden

Free yourselves of everything that you find, both within and outside of you – religion, tradition and society –, for only thus will you find liberation. If you are not entangled in things, unimpeded, you will reach independence.
  Zen Master Lin-Chi (ninth century)

1

The Directness Of Zen

Zen is the height and the quintessence of the whole of Buddhism. It is the direct, immediate way to liberation from imprisonment within the circle of birth and death.

Zen is solely interested in the pure, unadulterated truth in itself. In the eyes of Zen, all religious systems and philosophical teachings are nothing more than mind-bending speculation and a heap of intellectual rubbish, and therefore devoid of all value.

The truth of Zen is astoundingly simple and its methods of conveyance are constantly and uncompromisingly direct:

> A Zen student goes to Zen Master Hsing-hua and says, "Master, I am deeply confused, I no longer even know the difference between black and white. What do you say to that?" The old master says, "What did you say? Come a little closer, my hearing is so poor today."
> The student steps a little closer and repeats himself: "I do not know what the difference is between black and white."
> Hardly has he finished speaking when he receives a resounding slap to the ear. This leads the monk to a sudden insight and, filled with gratitude, he bows before his master.

Why make everything so complicated? The truth is, it is all very simple. But exactly because it is so simple, you make everything so complicated. The reason for this is that you are used to doing everything with your head. Yet behind every answer you find, a new question will instantly appear. You believe that everything of value for you in life must be achieved through great activity and effort. However, in Zen there is nothing to achieve – truly nothing.

"Tao lies directly beneath the soles of your feet", as the Chinese masters of old say. Simply look and you will see that it has always been here. It has always been here – yet you are not here! "Now", in this moment, the reality of your true being reveals itself "here".

If you cannot find it here you will not find it anywhere. Zen Master Lin-chi, the Dharma successor of Huang-po, says:

> You wear down your feet rushing in all directions, what are you seeking? There is no buddha to seek, nor is there a way to perfect, nor a universal truth to attain.

No sooner do you hear of Enlightenment, of the exalted teachings of Buddhism, of the sacred truth beyond the insipid, profane world, than you start your search. Yet Zen tells you, "That there is nothing to be reached are not empty words but the highest truth." It is paradoxical that the truth has always been present and attainable yet it withdraws itself as soon as you deliberately try to grasp it. The truth of Zen is directly before you but as soon as you start reflecting on it you are mistaken.

When you interpret things with your intellect you distance yourself more and more from the truth of Zen. Zen can never be made the object of logical deliberations and explanations. Instead, to truly understand its truth, you must live it within you at your innermost. You can never comprehend a thought unless it is supported by your own experience.

If you do not grasp this, and believe that you can comprehend the profound truth of Zen with your intellect, you will only end up in blocking your path to liberation. You will just be searching in circles. You search and analyse, prodding here and there in the hope of finding something after all. You believe that somewhere out there, there is indeed a great philosophical realisation which will come from outwards and make the matter clear. Yet the result is that you become increasingly caught up in the creeping tangle of your discriminating, conceptual thinking. But Zen rises above all this and calls to you:

> If you could only free yourself from conceptual thinking you would know that there is no other buddha than the one in your own mind.

These words by Zen Master Huang-po (ninth century) form the core of true, original Zen of the ancient Chinese masters. Only when you can prevent your thoughts from roaming and searching are you truly on the Zen path to liberation. For when you try to grasp Zen with concepts, you create your own restrictions and shut out reality.

You limit yourself to within your self-produced confinements of dualistic discrimination. Each thought produces the next one and thus you distance yourself ever more. The more you become caught in the entwinement of your discriminating thought, the further away you are from the truth you seek. "All thought is an erroneous belief", says Zen. Why stuff your brain with all sorts of intellectual rubbish? What is the point of rooting around in every corner like a dog who scrapes up nothing but old rubbish in its muzzle? Dig into your own treasure, for the truth you are seeking is closer to you than you are to yourself.

There is nothing to seek and there is nothing to gain! There is no space in which things could be separate from one another, and there is no time in which anything is yet to happen or has already taken place. For everything is a simultaneity, revealing itself in this instance "now-here".

This, too, is the central thought behind the Hua-yen school of Chinese Buddhism, based on the Avatamsaka Sutra. The fundament of the Hua-yen school is "the teaching of the mutual pervasiveness of all things" – the teaching of the fundamental unity, entirety, and equity of all beings. The whole universe is an integral organism, a cosmic network, in which everything is mutually pervading and is mutually connected. To better illustrate this, the Avatamsaka Sutra uses the analogy of Indra's pearl net.

Here it is said that high up in the heavens, above the palace of the god Indra, there is a great net made up of an endless number of pearls. All the pearls in this net are so strung that each pearl reflects all others. Thus, a single pearl contains all the others and, by reflections of the light, simultaneously reflects the whole cosmos and all that it contains.

Everything is an all-embracing wholeness, containing everything within itself. Everything is an absolute Here and Now. Since now-here everything is present, where will you seek and what will you seek? Now is here and here is now! If you wish to experience your true being you must immerse yourself in it "now, here". How do you hope to experience "now" if you are caught up with tomorrow or the day after – when you are elsewhere?

The transitory nature of all being can suddenly and unexpectedly shatter all your speculations. Everything you are planning for the future is a speculation with a particular goal, yet faced with the presence of death it is nothing at all, absolutely worthless. In the words of Zen Master Yung-chia (eighth century):

> The matter of life and death is immense and impermanence swiftly grasps hold. How can you waste your time with trivialities?

Nothing is important in the face of the presence of death! Let go of everything, whatever it may be – "MU" – nothing! MU is nothingness in terms of space and time, and thus nothingness with regards to all content of consciousness.

MU is here-now and reveals itself "now-here". There is no coming and there is no going. MU is all-encompassing, be it behind, in front, above, below, and to the side, it is everywhere. This MU is "now" – and this "now" is eternity. Realise this and immerse yourself in it!

Your mind will then be completely free, even though it moves within the realm of life and death. You no longer embroil yourself in empty fantasies and the vanities of material desires. Free from attachments to the world of the senses, nothing can deceive you any longer. You live unbound in the midst of the world and pass through birth and death in complete freedom. You come and go as you please and are completely free and independent.

In Chinese Zen painting we often encounter Hotei, known in Zen as the "laughing buddha". Hotei is usually depicted as a small fat man with a large sack slung over his shoulder and an infectiously broad smile covering his face. This laughing buddha represents the one who is totally liberated, having broken through all boundaries and transcended the world. He embodies the highest ideal of Zen as portrayed in the last of the Ten Ox-herding Pictures.

Hotei lived during the Tang dynasty, the golden age of Zen Buddhism in China. He was a Zen master of highest spiritual fulfilment, yet he had no desire whatsoever to live in a monastery and instruct disciples. Instead, he wandered through the villages with a sack over his shoulder and handed out sweets to the children.

Hotei lived the life of a Zen tramp, unattached and independent. Like the wind in the trees and the moon on the water he lived his life in total freedom, in accordance with the universe.

> One day Hotei met a Zen monk who asked him, "What is the secret of Zen?"
> Hotei's silent response was to let the sack he was carrying on his back fall to the ground and to spread out his arms.
> "Then tell me", asked the monk, "what is the essence of Zen realisation?"
> The "laughing buddha" immediately grabbed his sack, slung it over his shoulder, and continued on his way without looking back.

The freedom and cheerfulness of Mind is the natural state of your being. Simply free your mind of everything, whatever it may be. If you just take each situation as it arises, you will be in complete concordance with everything. Zen Master Lin-chi tells us this too:

> The true path of Zen is very simple and requires no effort. It is found in everyday life and is without aim: dressing oneself, pissing, shitting, eating, and sleeping when one is tired. The ignorant ones, without Zen intuition, may laugh at me but the wise ones understand.

These words from one of the most original masters in the history of Zen are bound to shock certain people and they will ask themselves: how can this be the true Zen Way? Yet the old master Lao-tse would call down from his ox, "True words are not pleasant and pleasant words are not true."

Zen is always refreshingly direct and does not digress in pleasant words and friendly fussings, aimed at uplifting the ego.

> One day, a monk came to Zen Master Tokusan (ninth century) to ask him about the truth of Zen. In accordance with Buddhist regulations he bowed deeply before his master prior to asking his question. But before he had finished bowing, Tokusan gave him a violent blow with the stick.
> "Why are you hitting me?" asked the monk, with a pain-distorted face, "I haven't said anything yet".
> "There would be no point in waiting for you to open your mouth", said Tokusan and raised his

stick, ready for the next blow. The monk quickly took leave.

Zen has but one sole concern. It wishes to thoroughly destroy all your attachments to words, ideas, and expectations, so that you awaken from your dreaming. That is why Zen Master Huang-po says:

> Students of the way, if you do not awaken to this mind-substance you will cover the mind with conceptual thinking, seek buddha outside of yourselves, and remain attached to forms, pious exercises and such like, which is detrimental and has nothing to do with the way to highest realisation.

Why are you unable to recognise your original being although it is always present? Why do you hold on to artificially constructed spiritual practices and teachings which are devoid of all value and mere pastimes of the ego? Why build a discussion on false concepts?

Some of you have been asked the question of what I teach you. I shall tell you: my teaching is the teaching that there is nothing to teach. It is "the Freedom of Zen", the truth beyond all words and limitations, whatever they may be. Immerse yourself "now" this very instant in the present moment, and see things as they really are. Be independent of everything, whatever it is! Free yourself of everything – above all of yourself, and in a flash you will achieve all-encompassing realisation.

Once, a very highbrow theologian came to my master Soji Enku and said, "I heard your last lecture but I am still not clear on the facts of Zen. I would therefore like to ask you: what constitutes the fundamental truth of Zen?" Soji Enku simply replied, "The ground beneath your feet – that is the fundamental truth of Zen." The highbrow theologian can call himself lucky that my master, in his grandmotherly goodness, answered him in such a friendly way. If he had asked one of the old Chinese masters of the early days, like Tokusan, Lin-chi, or Ma-tsu, he would surely have been instantly struck to the ground.

> Once, a monk asked Zen Master Ma-tsu: "What is the reason for Bodhidharma's (the first Zen patriarch's) coming from the west?" Immediately, the master gave him such a violent blow to the chest that the monk fell to the ground.
> Ma-tsu laughed loudly and bellowed, "If I had not struck you down, the whole land would have laughed at me!"

Such an original, direct, and spontaneous teaching method lifts the intellect from its hinges and short-circuits the process of thinking. Zen points constantly and with great emphasis to the direct experience of pure truth, and does not burden itself with conjectures and empty talk.

Without doubt, the main characteristic of Zen is its incomprehensibility. Like water which flows through your fingers, it eludes all conceptual classification. Everything is perfectly clear, yet your discriminating, conceptual thought makes it unclear. As long as you are a prisoner of your intellectualness and try to interpret things using reasoning, you will never find entry to the truth of Zen.

While we are on the subject of Soji Enku, I'd like to tell you about one other little situation I experienced with him. One afternoon, a number of students were tidying up Soji Enku's room and were busy talking about this and that. The master was sitting at his desk and slowly turned himself on his swivel-chair to the left and right, and appeared to be completely indifferent to what was happening.

Suddenly, he stopped with a jolt, pointed to the wall and said, "What is that nasty spot there? Where has that suddenly appeared from?" Everyone looked and asked, "What spot?" – "Over there on the wall. Can't you see it?"

All at once he removed his glasses and said in great surprise, "Oh, it's gone." Then he put his glasses back on and said, "I say, now it's back again." He then examined his glasses and said, "Oh, what is that spot on my glasses?" Afterwards, everyone was sheepish and quiet. Each of them had understood the wonderful lesson.

Together they had filled the room with their individual projections of their identifications and misinterpretations. One idea confronted another idea, ignorance confronted ignorance. Much ado about nothing.

But in China, as far back as the fourth century, the Taoist Master Chuang-tse said:

> Far better than to counter another's every "yes" with a "no" and every "no" with a "yes" is the way of Enlightenment.

"Yes" and "no", affirmation and negation are born of ignorance, this being the way it usually manifests itself. As long as you still dwell in a logical, dualistic state of ignorance and you continue to cling to your own prejudices, you are condemned to squirm in the straitjacket of your own projections.

You are caught in maya, the illusion of a world of deception that you dream, which is a phenomenon that has no reality of its own. Thus, there is no other way than to leave everything just as it is and awaken. Only in this way can you become a master who shatters all limits and bounds. In other words, free yourself of everything and your true self, which is constantly present and has always been so, will radiate clear and bright a hundred thousand times brighter than the sun.

Enlightenment is not something that comes in from the outside. Many people think they could be sitting here now in their ignorance and suddenly, a light would shine forth, like a light bulb, and everything would become clear.

The truth of it is, the projections you have been projecting onto reality your whole life long and longer still will vanish. Then everything is just as it is and as it has always been. Then you will experience that there was never anything like birth and death, or space and time, and thus there is no external world of phenomena, bound by space and time. All these are mere phenomena of the maya-dream, which you yourself dream – projections resulting from ignorance.

Enlightenment and ignorance, imprisonment in the circle of birth, ageing, despair, illness, pain, and death – all belong to the dream you are dreaming. Therefore, there is only one possibility to escape from this, and that is: Wake up! Awaken and stop dreaming!

(short silence)

Should I say more? Or should I say no more? If I say nothing more you might start believing that everything has been said about the Truth. Yet if I say more, there is the danger you will believe there is something to be said about the highest Truth, which is beyond all words. But no word hits the mark! Everything that I just said has nothing to do with it. Everything that has ever been expressed about God, Enlightenment, or eternal life etcetera, is nothing more than utter rubbish. It has nothing whatsoever to do with the inexpressible reality which is beyond everything that sense and reason can comprehend. "So why take autumn leaves for gold?"

All religious and philosophical sayings are like an empty fist which one holds out to a child for fun. The child believes there is something in it – but there is nothing. No spiritual system holds the truth. You can seek as long as you like. You can spend your whole life studying every religious and philosophical teaching there is. But none of this has anything to do with the inexpressible truth. Therefore, I shall give you this piece of advice: let it all go! Free yourself of everything! Do not needlessly waste your time. Think of the admonishing words of Yun-men:

> Do not needlessly waste your time! Once you have lost your human corpus you will not regain one for innumerable aeons to come. That is no trifle.
> Do not rely on external things. When even a worldly man such as Confucius could once say, "When I hear of Tao in the morning I can die in peace in the evening" – how much more is this valid for us Zen monks? So what is the problem

that needs to be dealt with? Above all, you must make great efforts! Take heed of this!

All things are like a dream, a vision, petals from nowhere; to chase after them is a completely pointless and arduous exercise. A true person of Zen views all phenomena on his path through the world as illusion. He is constantly master of himself and does not make himself slave to human passions. Free of all identifications, in the turmoil of the world he breaks through to the clear light of reality.

2

The Highest Truth Is Not Difficult

The highest truth is not difficult and allows no preferences.
When you cease wanting or hating, it reveals itself clearly and infinitely. Yet whoever remains separated by even a hair's breadth is so far from it like the heavens from the earth.
ZEN MASTER SENG-TSAN (SEVENTH CENTURY)

"The highest truth is not difficult", says Zen Master Seng-tsan. What do you make of that? In order to even learn a foreign language you have to make an effort. But to attain the Utmost, something of such gigantic proportions that my words are not enough to proclaim it to you – that should be without the slightest difficulty?

Yet let me tell you this: not only is the highest truth not difficult, but it is in fact the easiest thing in the world. But if you search for it in books, everything becomes very complicated and difficult.

You are seriously convinced that Zen is a toilsome matter. The truth is, however, it is very simple, yet your intellect cannot imagine how simple it is. For this reason you convince yourself that it must be very difficult, but it is only difficult due to the wrong preconceptions with which you approach it.

The wrong preconceptions are that you are searching for something that you can never find, however hard you try, since that which you are seeking is constantly present as your innermost possession.

That is why Zen Master Da-zhu (eighth century) says:

> The treasure house within you contains everything and is entirely at your disposal. You do not need to seek beyond it.

What you are seeking is your true, divine self, beyond space and time, and beyond birth and death. It is your true reality. You have never lost it, it is always there. It is just that you have covered it with the projections of your deluded thoughts. The highest truth you are seeking is directly before you and reveals itself in all forms and all appearances.

> One day, a monk came to the Chinese Zen Master Tsao-shan (ninth century) and asked him: "What of the appearances is true?"
> Tsao-shan said, "Appearance is truth and truth is appearance."
> The monk did not understand and continued, "And where does it reveal itself?"
> "Here!", said the master, raising the tea tray into the air.

Everything is reality. Everything is a revelation of the truth. Nothing exists which is not a manifestation of the truth. And yet you smother reality with your notion of multiplicity and separateness. If you ask me, "Where does reality reveal itself?", I could perhaps refer to this gong. I could also point to this lamp or to this picture. Everything that you perceive is reality, the highest truth, just as it is.

The highest truth is not difficult and allows no preferences.

This "*no preferences*" would be, for example, if you say, "Here I am in beautiful surroundings, sitting by the sea, listening to the sound of the surf, smelling the wonderful salty air, hearing the cry of the seagulls – fantastic – this is a spiritual dimension." And then on the other hand you say, "Now I am in a sleazy night bar with naked dancing girls, the smell of alcohol, and cheap perfume – this is the world of desire, this cannot be the truth." Yet that is exactly the meaning of "making preferences", which becomes your undoing.

The path I teach you is the "Tantric Zen Way". This great Zen Way is not a way for small, limited minds. It is the path to Enlightenment in the midst of the world, in the midst of life's daily demands. I have spoken of this at length in my book "The Great Zen Way".

You can never find liberation by withdrawing yourself from the world to live in a monastery, just singing holy songs and sitting on your meditation cushion, staring at the wall, mindlessly as cattle. The Tantric Zen Way is the way of the "fire lotus". It is the direct way to liberation, whilst preserving inner stability and serenity in the midst of external distractions.

This active Zen Way requires a decisive strong will, such that you retain your unshakeability of mind in all difficulties and joys of daily life. Whoever retreats from the world and then clings to this retreating, and is unable to live in the realm of passions without coming to harm, will neither be able to save himself nor others.

I would not point you along this way if I had not gone along it myself. My way to Enlightenment is completely out of the ordinary and is in no way in keeping with the generally accepted idea of a path to liberation. But I do not need to go into that here – you all know my story. Everywhere, no matter where, is the reality that you seek.

In the words of the apostle Paul, "Everything is filled with the fullness of God." Everywhere, the glory of the divine being reveals itself. If you do not find it in the midst of daily life, in the world of desire, then you will also not find it in a Buddhist temple, a church or in any other "holy" place. Then it is just another illusion created by your conditioned, discriminating thought, and you only end up in fooling yourself. That is why Zen Master Lin-chi says:

> While you love what is holy and loath what is common, you are still bobbing up and down in the sea of ignorance.

You must rise above both of these – the profane and the sacred! Free yourself of every discrimination – you must not cling to anything!

> A monk once asked Master Tsao-shan, the master with the tea tray: "Who wields the sword in this empire?"
> Zen Master Tsao-shan said, "I do! I, Tsao-shan wield the sword in my hand!"
> And the monk asked, "Whom do you intend to kill with it?"
> "Everyone!" said the Master.
> "But what if you were to encounter your parents, would you kill them too?"

"Why make an exception for them?" said the Master.
"All right", said the monk, "but you would still be left over."
"What is to be done then?" asked the Master.
"You could kill yourself!" said the monk.
Tsao-chan replied, "I would not know where to begin."

This is absolute "non-discrimination". Neither accepting nor rejecting. That is why Zen Master Lin-chi also says: "You have yet to take leave of the family!" What he means is: you still have not left behind your conditionings, patterns of behaviour, and modes of thought.

You continue to be a prisoner of all your stencils and fixations, and you are yet to abide in the cloudless clarity of the Mind, and thus you remain trapped in discriminating thought. In his work Hsin-hsin-ming, the "Seal of Faith", Zen Master Seng-ts'an further says:

When you cease wanting or hating, the truth reveals itself clearly and infinitely.

When you are free of wanting and hating, which means of accepting and rejecting, attachment and aversion, the highest truth reveals itself clearly and infinitely. It reveals itself when you no longer differentiate or make preferences.

Yin and yang belong together and complement one another. You cannot have one without the other. It would be just like wanting to have an electric current with no minus pole, just the plus pole. Or like wanting the sun to shine every day and never have rain again. Everything is the one reality; be it a pretty butterfly, be it a beautiful flower, or be it a pile of stinking dog shit on the road.

> A Zen student asked his master: "Who is the buddha of all buddhas of the past, present, and future?"
> "The yarrow bush behind the shit house."

Why differentiate? Everything is one, for everything is an organic, all-encompassing whole, containing everything within itself – there is nothing you can remove. You can remove nothing, not even a speck of dust.

If you were able to remove anything from the universe – be it but a speck of dust – the entire universe would collapse. Even when you split an atom in a laboratory, this splitting merely transforms it into another form of energy. You cannot destroy anything, dissolve it, or make it disappear – you can only transform it.

Everything is the great Tantra – the great transformation. That is why Zen is about being in harmony with this all-encompassing transformation of the Tao. The entire universe is in constant motion. Be one with this motion, do not oppose it, and you will find yourself in Tao!

Simply do not differentiate, and you will see that everything is good, just as it is. Were it not so, that too would be good.

I know it is not easy to accept this truth, but in the end you have no alternative but to accept it – not in pessimistic resignation, but through inner insight. You can experience the world as a wonderful paradise, or you can experience it as hell, it is all up to you.

At the last Zen sesshin I told you of the encounter between Zen Master Hakuin and a Samurai:

> A samurai comes to Zen Master Hakuin and says: "The question of heaven and hell has been bothering me for a long time. Therefore, I would like to ask you: is there really such a thing as paradise and hell?"
> Hakuin says, "Who are you to just come along and ask me such a question?"
> "Can't you see? I'm a samurai of the Imperial Guard!" replies the samurai, full of pride.
> Hakuin starts to laugh and says, "Impossible, our emperor would never engage such a wretched-looking character as you. You look like a miserable beggar to me."
> Filled with rage, the samurai reaches for his sword, wrenches it out and charges towards Hakuin.
> Hakuin raises his hand and says in a calm voice, "The gates to hell have just opened." As if struck by lightening, the samurai stops, puts his sword away, and bows to Hakuin.
> Hakuin then says, "The gates to paradise have just opened."

You alone project this entire theatre-world, this entire dream world, just as you perceive it. This is also true for all you experience in bardo, the intermediate state between death and rebirth, as reported in the Tibetan Book of the Dead. All of it is projections of samsaric consciousness. This holds for all of the wrathful buddhas and all other frightening figures, as well as for the beautifully radiating, peaceful buddhas that appear in the vision of bardo. They are no more than unrestrained projections of consciousness.

Therefore, it is very important that you acquire "awareness of Mind" and "non-discriminating clarity" in the midst of daily life. It is absolutely necessary for you to see through the deceptive nature of all phenomena during all activities, wherever they may be, so that everywhere, including bardo, you can recognise all phenomena as your own projections. For just as you project phenomena in everyday life, you also project them in the intermediate state between death and rebirth. The process is one and the same; there is not the slightest difference.

The moment you recognise all phenomena as your own projections you will experience your ascent above the dark haze of phenomena into the clear light of reality. Your true eye of the Enlightened Mind is suddenly opened and, like one who has risen from the dead, you break out in laughter and clap your hands in sheer joy.

In that instant you realise that your own mind and the boundless expanse of the One Mind are a single being, beside which nothing exists.

Whoever remains separated from reality by even a hair's breadth is so far from it like the heavens from the earth.

"The smallest is the same as the biggest, and the biggest is the same as the smallest", says Lao-tse. It is the same here. When you draw your bow string and aim at a target but the arrow misses, then you have missed, be it by a hair's breadth or a metre; it makes no difference. The difference is great in any case. Free yourself of the slavery of discriminating, conceptual thought. For every deviation from the non-discriminating clarity of the Mind, however small it may be, separates you infinitely from absolute reality.

> One day, a monk came to Zen Master Tsao-shan and requested, "Master, I am sick, please heal me."
> Tsao-shan said, "I will not heal you."
> "Why not?" asked the monk.
> Tsao-shan replied, "So that you neither live nor die."

"Neither live nor die!" HO! (At this instant Zensho hits the gong's metal frame with a wooden stick!!!) Where does this HO belong to – to life or to death? Whatever you say has nothing to do with the issue at hand.

Only once you surpass it does it reveal itself. Then we will stand eye to eye and every further word will be superfluous. So why build a discussion on false concepts?

> Once, Zen Master Tokusan came into the monk's hall, raised his staff and said, "If you have any word to say, I will give you thirty blows with my staff. Should you have no word to say, you will also receive thirty blows all over your skull."

Accepting and rejecting, right and wrong, good and bad, worldly or spiritual: all this is the struggle of discriminating, conceptual thought.

The worldly exists only when you distinguish between worldly and spiritual; the spiritual reveals itself only when you cease clinging to the spiritual. When your mind is pure and empty, then all things are pure and empty. Then you can abide in the ordinary world and yet be completely independent. When you have fulfilled this, you are free like the wind in the trees and the birds in the air. As master of all situations you become one with all the various circumstances. Without hindrances and limitations you are as vast and as open as boundless space and you live "The Freedom of Zen" in the midst of the world.

(short silence)

When I pause for a while as I just did, some of you may start to think: "Let's see what comes now." But I tell you: it is already here! Everything that could possibly come is already here. There is nothing to wait for. From the very beginning on not a single blade of grass has stirred, the true Word has already been spoken. When you are here, it is here! Everything that is here is also elsewhere and what is not here is nowhere.

> A novice came to Zen Master Nansen (ninth century) and said, "Master, I am new at the monastery and I seek the way to Enlightenment. Please advise me how to find it."
> Master Nansen asked, "Do you hear the rush of the river?"
> "Yes, Master."
> "That is the way", said the Master.

And so I ask you: Do you hear the sound of the rain?

3

Stop Searching

Students of the way, if you wish to become buddha, you need not study any doctrine; you must only learn how to avoid seeking and attaching yourselves to anything.
ZEN MASTER HUANG-PO (NINTH CENTURY)

These few words from the Chinese Zen Master Huang-po are pure Zen. They are perfectly clear-spoken words of highest insight.

Yet it is complete nonsense when Huang-po says, "Students of the way, if you wish to become buddha". How can we wish to become something we already are? How can we wish to gain something we already have and have eternally had as our most inherent being?

And yet what Huang-po says is entirely correct. Yet since you believe you have lost it and must regain it, he gives you this well-meant advice, "Students of the way, if you wish to become buddha, you need not study any doctrine."

Thus, one of the errors has been eliminated. The belief that you must become buddha, an enlightened being, is your first error because from the very beginning you have always been the true buddha. When you further believe you must study a certain philosophy or religion – an artificially created system of thought – in order to become enlightened, then you have your second error. It is of the utmost importance to recognise that in truth, there is nothing to attain. Absolutely nothing!

The true, basic nature of your being is the incomprehensible, radiating nature of the One Mind. Yet since you do not recognise the cause of birth and death, you take that to be true which is in fact false, and cling on tightly to it. In mindless routine you follow erroneous ways, thus binding yourself to birth and death, and experiencing all sorts of suffering.

In truth, the Mind is filled with radiant clarity. And thus, cast off the darkness of your old, dead concepts – free yourself of everything! "That there is nothing to be attained are not empty words but the highest truth", says Huang-po. There are no doctrines you need to study. This is the fundamental prerequisite for a comprehension of Zen. That is why Zen Master Lin-chi says:

> Friends of Zen, I say to you: There is no Buddha and no doctrine, no instruction and no realisation. What are you chasing after so embitteredly? Why do you wish to set another head on top of your own, you blind blockheads? What are you lacking?
>
> Whoever is in unison with the Tao is no different from the buddhas and patriarchs. But you do not trust in your inner wisdom and so you turn your search to the outside. Do not let yourselves be deceived!
>
> The highest truth is nothing you can find in the external world. Instead of clinging to my words you should become calm and stop your external searching. Do not stick to the past and do not cling to the future either! That is much better than spending many years searching around in vain.

You must only learn how to avoid seeking and attaching yourselves to anything.

Learning that there is nothing to learn and nothing to seek is true learning in the spirit of Zen. Where nothing is sought, the Unborn Mind is present. It is also constantly present whilst you are seeking it. Yet precisely due to your seeking and brooding, you cover it with the dark clouds of your discriminating ignorance. That is why Zen Master Huang-long (twelfth century) says:

> When your mind is still, there is no ruminative brooding. If you do not deliberately practise the Way, you follow it step by step. Where there is no brooding there is no world to be transcended. If you do not deliberately practise the Way, there is no Way that you could seek.

The moment you stop seeking, the reality of your original condition of Mind will shine forth and light up the boundless universe with its immeasurable radiance. But as long as you continue seeking, as long as you are prey to the erroneous assumption of there being something to find, be it even as tiny as a speck of dust, you fall into the realm of duality. You fall into the realm of affirmation and negation, of distinguishing between right and wrong, and you entangle yourself ever more in the circle of birth and death.

This dualistic state of mind is the true cause of samsara. It spawns all your habitual thoughts and keeps all deceptive notions alive. The radiating, untarnished One Mind will only reveal itself when the mind has been purified of the creeping tangle of discriminating, conceptual thinking. That is why Zen Master Huang-po says:

> Being entirely without concepts
> is the wisdom of non-attachment.
> Where there is no attachment
> the indestructible Mind is present.

The counterpart of attachment is letting go. Therefore it would be reasonable for you to say, "Alright, I shall make an effort to let go." However, this type of letting go is not the letting go of Zen. It does not correspond to the attitude of mind of wu-wei, nondoing, and wu-nien, nonthinking. Rather, it is just the desire to let go, an activity of the ego. This desire causes inner tension, for tension is always impeded desire.

Therefore, attachment cannot be undone through its counterpart of letting go when you "do" it. All opposites, being and nonbeing, life and death, coming and going, right and wrong, belong to the dualistic realm of ignorance.

To make this distinction clear, I would like to tell you about an encounter between a monk and Zen Master Joshu (ninth century).

> A monk came to Zen Master Joshu and said, "Look, I have let go of everything. Nothing is left in my consciousness. What do you say to that?" Joshu unexpectedly replied, "Then throw it away!" The monk was most astonished, and thought that old Joshu could not have understood him due to his old age, so he repeated with emphasis, "But master, I just told you that I have let go of

everything. What is left for me to throw away?"
To this Joshu replied, "Well, if that is so, you will just have to carry it further."

The old master's reply has the sharpness of a samurai sword. But the monk was clinging too much to his notion of having let go. Therefore, Joshu's blow with the sword was sadly unable to bring him to life. The letting go you "do" becomes a pseudo letting go that holds you back.

You are a prisoner of your "self-made" letting go, stuck in your notion of having let go. However: "Only where there is no attachment is the indestructible Mind present." This is where the clear light of reality shines forth.

Countless teachings and methods exist as philosophies or religious disciplines, such as performing prostrations, kundalini meditation, sutra recitation, to name but a few. The esoteric fairground offers many methods which promise the spiritual seeker wonderful visions, mystical ecstasy, and powers to perform miracles. Yet all this belongs to the world of dreams and hot air. They are but signs and miracles to dazzle the ignorant. That is why I say again and again, "Esotericism is only for dimwits."

All these artificial methods and doctrines that are supposed to work against delusion amount to no more than an illusion – puffs of air in empty space. There is nothing to be attained and there is no sacred truth to be fulfilled. Even the slightest notion that something can be attained is once again delusion.

People often come here and ask me, "What is your teaching?" – I do not proclaim any defined teaching!

Here, just as in true original Chinese Zen, there is no teaching. Many guests who come to our public Zen sesshins only want to hear things which are comforting, and above all congenial. They are not bothered about the truth itself. They just want to be comforted and go home contented. They come, hoping to receive a particular teaching, something they can cling on to.

One thing should not be forgotten here, I am no religious teacher, no theologian, and no philosopher, but a Zen master. And a Zen master never gives anything to anybody – because there is nothing to be given. I only heal afflictions and undo bonds. All you could be given are dead ideas and empty words, which are utterly useless to you.

What is really of value is what you already have since it is already there within you as your innermost self. Only a truly enlightened Master can open your inner eye, so that your focus turns inwards and you recognise your true self. Thus, I use all means at my disposal to make you turn your attention inwards, such that you recognise what has always been there within you.

I do not impart borrowed doctrines. Neither do I impart a "dusty dharma" in the form of precast, fixedly defined teachings. Quite the opposite is true. I call upon you: let go of all your dead doctrines! It's all just a load of rubbish!

I do not tell you, "Believe this and that." I say to you: Have faith! Have faith in the all-fulfilling and all-sustaining truth of the One Mind, beside which nothing exists! It is your true being, unborn and indestructible. Do not seek it, do not name it, and do not confine it!

Be as vast and as open as the sky and the One Mind reveals itself as your original, true being. Put all religious and philosophical doctrines into question! They are nothing other than the interpretations of a neurotic intellect. You do not need to believe in any religious dogma. Free yourself of your conditioned notion that you must believe in something! When you question everything, whatever it may be, and as far as you can go, sooner or later the truth will reveal itself just as it is. It is the truth that lies beyond everything that sense and reason can comprehend.

When I speak of doubt, I do not, however, mean this "intellectual doubt" of those intellectual pseudo-Zenists who doubt everything except their ego. Rather, I mean that particular form of doubt that, in the end, doubts itself, so that it becomes doubt without content. This is a pure perception of doubt, known in Zen as the "Great Doubt".

The Great Doubt is an inescapable state of mind which always precedes the Enlightenment experience. It is a form of mental obstruction, in which the flow of thoughts blocks and is unable to continue. The endless abyss of the divine void opens before you and you stand on the threshold of mystical death. In this situation of the Great Doubt Zen calls to you:

> At the edge of the abyss, let go of everything and die completely, then return to life – nothing more can deceive you now.

As long as you still trust in external teachings and borrowed doctrines, you are still far away from the abyss of the divine void. You are bound by the delusions of your discriminating, conceptual thought and you have confined yourself. Every teaching is a danger to the free mind. All teachings are dangerous as they become dogmas and enchain the mind. Furthermore, your preoccupation with all sorts of teachings and artificial methods only leads to you wasting your precious time and squandering your spiritual energy. There is nothing to learn and nothing to gain. Whoever believes there is something to seek is like a blind man in a dark room searching for a black cat which does not exist. The Chinese masters of old constantly referred with utmost emphasis to the fact that there is nothing to learn and nothing to be gained on the Zen way. Zen Master Huang-po thus says:

> The many methods which are meant to work against the many forms of illusion are no more than sayings which are there to draw in people to the gates of liberation. In reality, none of them is of any substance.

Letting go of everything is the highest truth. Whoever grasps this is a buddha. Letting go of all illusion then leaves no teaching behind upon which you can find support.

When you suddenly realise the fact that your own mind is the divine truth which you are seeking, and that there is nothing to achieve, and that there is no deed for you to perform – you then have the highest realisation!

This means fulfilling your buddha-nature and becoming buddha yourself, which you already are at the base of your being. Yet all the countless number of methods which are supposed to bring people to the gates of liberation belong too to the realm of delusion.

The "door-less door" to liberation has no door since it is constantly present. "Here and now" it manifests itself in its entire magnificence. To experience this, you need solely let go of everything this instant, whatever it may be, and thus forget yourself and all things. By dying into the abyss of the divine void you will rise above the dark mists of phenomena into the clear light of Reality.

In this boundless liberation nothing remains to be done. There is no longer any special religious practise to be performed, no dharma, and no spiritual ordinance to fulfil. There is nothing more you could use to lean on for the simple reason that you no longer need anything to lean on – you no longer need crutches.

"Take up thy bed and walk!" says Jesus to the lame man. The lame man is the one who has lost his reality, forgotten who he is, and is no longer able to free himself from the attractions of the world because of his earth-binding identification with temporal things. He lies on the earth and cannot rise. And Jesus says to him: "Rise, take up thy bed and walk!"

This means relinquishing all delusion; it is total liberation. This is how you rise above all your conditionings, the result of your identification with the entwined memories of a dead past.

Once you have the courage to let go of everything and leave everything as it is, in that instant, the reality of what you really are will shine forth. Once you were lame; now you can walk again. Once you were blind; now your eyes have been opened. You will transcend the whole universe and be free from birth and death.

4

When The Soap Bubble Bursts

All buddhas and all sentient beings are nothing but the One Mind, besides which nothing exists.
ZEN MASTER HUANG-PO (NINTH CENTURY)

This statement by the Chinese Zen Master Huang-po shatters all conventional, rational thinking. With one yank it pulls the floor out from under your feet. Everything to which you are accustomed and all that is familiar to you is radically thrown into question by this core statement of Zen.

Many a time we have used the illustration of soap bubbles in empty space. It is a very useful aid for making things a little clearer.

The endless expanse of the heavens is the one space, the one sole reality, and within this space we imagine a multitude of soap bubbles floating around. These iridescent soap bubbles, which we experience as external form, we shall consider as sentient beings.

Whether there now be a hundred, a thousand, or a million soap bubbles in the endless expanse of the heavens, we still cannot say there actually exists a multitude of individual spaces within the soap bubbles.

Every spatial discrimination and separation is just illusory. In reality, there is only the one endless expanse of the heavens. But each soap bubble, due to its state of ignorance caused by the obscuration of the mind, believes itself to be in possession of its own inner space, and experiences itself as a separate individual, separate from all other soap bubbles. The endless heavens surrounding the soap bubble and the space within the soap bubble do not differ in any way. It is just that the heavens – the endless expanse of the One Mind – is divided into inner and outer, unity and multiplicity by the arbitrary limitations of the intellect.

This multiplicity is, however, no more than a delusion, because everything we perceive with our senses which looks so stable in form has no substance of its own. We can also view the soap bubbles in terms of the five skandhas. These individual elements of existence that give rise to the delusion of a personality are classified into five groups, according to Buddhist teaching. They are listed in order of decreasing density as: corporeality, sensation, perception, mental formations, and consciousness.

We relate all these to the soap bubble's round form, its colours, its surface tension and so on. Together, these factors produce an apparent whole, and densify to the illusion of form, space, and time, such that you believe this to be your personality, along with the world you experience. And so you float back and forth, lost like soap bubbles in space, and are convinced that this is your true being. However, this personality does not have a true being, it is merely an event. It is nothing more than a mere process of mental and physical phenomena.

You can analyse it as much as you want; the structure of the bubbles, the surface tension, and the various colour transitions.

You can make hundreds of therapies, study philosophies and busy yourself with all sorts of esoteric lunacy – all this you can do but in the end, the bubble's substance remains unchanged – absolutely unchanged!

Therefore: ... (Zensho strikes his staff on the floor!!!)

Die and be completely dead! Then do whatever you want and everything is good.

The soap bubble bursts when you see through the deceptive nature of all phenomena, fully placing your trust in the Almighty, and, having the courage to leave everything just as it is, surrender yourself in mystical death to the abyss of the divine void.

At this instant, the soap bubble bursts and nothing else exists than the sole, boundless expanse of space – the reality of the One Mind. You will experience yourself in your true unborn and immortal being, and will illuminate and fill the whole universe with the eternal blaze of the divine light which you yourself are.

Once you have recognised that the elements of existence which make up the delusion of a personality are not your true self, you no longer need fear their death – quite the contrary! The demise of the elements of existence would mean the ascent of the inner light of the one who is free of all identifications. To this Zen Master Huang-po says:

> If an ordinary man, when he is about to die, could only recognise the voidness of the five elements of existence and completely grasp that they do not constitute an "I"; and that the real Mind is formless and is neither coming nor going.
>
> If he could perceive that his nature is something neither commencing at birth nor perishing at his death, but is whole and motionless in its very depths, and that the Mind is one with all phenomena, he would receive Enlightenment in a flash.

This One Mind, which is your true self, is unborn and indestructible. Just as the expanse of outer space is indestructible, so too – returning to our illustration of the soap bubble – is the inner space of the soap bubble.

At the instant when the soap bubble dies – when it bursts – all that disappears is the outer shell. The only thing that dies is the process of an interplay of different factors that has created the perceived image of a shimmering soap bubble. And this had no being of its own to begin with.

Everything that is dependent on something else for its cause, as Buddha's teaching tells us, falls under the law of coming into being and passing away – and thus is transitory. But what is inside is the indestructible centre. It is that which obtains its being from itself. At the same time, this absolute centre is the all-encompassing totality that holds everything within it.

It is your true being, it has no beginning and does not end. That is why, when the Scribes and Pharisees asked Christ where he came from and who he was, he replied: "I am the Alpha and the Omega", meaning I embrace the beginning and the end – I am eternity!

Everything that has a beginning will at some point also have an end. But whatever is without beginning – the beginningless – will as a result have no end because this Mind, which has no beginning, is unborn and indestructible. It is neither this nor is it that, for Mind does not belong to the category of things that exist or do not exist. It is beyond all designation in the form of "being or nonbeing". Western philosophy says: "To be or not to be, that is the question!" But Zen views this in completely the opposite way. The Chinese Zen Master Yuan-wu says in the Pi-yen-lu, the Blue Cliff Record:

> Whoever reflects upon being or nonbeing loses life and limb!

When we say that the One Mind is neither this nor that, it means that it is beyond all contraries. As soon as a designation appears, be it just one term; when just a single thought appears, a second will follow. The moment something becomes fixed, its opposite will already have arisen of its own accord. That is why Lao-tse, the founding father of Taoism, says:

> When everyone knows: beauty is beautiful,
> then ugliness is already there.
> When everyone knows: goodness is good,
> then evil is already there.

Good and bad, yes and no, right and wrong are all manifestations of discriminating conceptual thought. This discriminating consciousness forms the basis of everything you experience. This is where the whole dream of a myriad dualistic phenomenal world arises. And you, as the dreamer, are caught in your own delusion of a cycle of birth and death, within the illusion of space and time.

It is as if you would have an endlessly long thread before you and would start playing with it. You pull at it here and there and wrap it a little around your finger, hand, and foot. You twist around and roll about on the floor with the thread in joy, and before you know it, you have become so entangled and trapped that you can no longer free yourself.

In this way you have created a net; a veil of maya and have become ensnared in it. Yet the more you try to use conceptual thought to free yourself from this self-made prison, this entanglement of discriminating conceptual thought, the more you ensnare yourself within it and are confused.

Behind this entire deception of a projecting consciousness is your true self – the One Mind. It is like a cinema screen on which all projections, images, forms, and movements take place. However, the Mind itself remains untouched, regardless of what happens. It has nothing whatsoever to do with all of this.

You are used to viewing your thoughts – all your projected concepts and notions – as being separate from the thinker. But this is a big mistake, a totally wrong point of view! The thinker is no more than the end effect of the interplay of the five elements of existence, the skandhas, which form the delusion of a personality.

The thinker is no more than the sum of the thoughts. In other words, he is the thinking itself. There is no thinker separate from the thinking, however much you may still believe you are a static, continuous entity. Essentially, there is nothing more than a rapid, complex succession of thoughts.

This sum of rapid, sequential thoughts arouses in you the deceptive impression of an individual consciousness which acts within the illusion of space and time. Since this space-time limited consciousness erroneously believes it is something that lies beyond the thoughts, beyond the perceptions, it regards itself as being the centre of this whole business. And exactly that is the constant process of formation and perpetuation of the delusion of an ego.

There is much talk today about the necessity of killing one's ego, the "I". However, this is an utterly false belief based on a complete lack of understanding. The truth is that no ego can be killed at all because, in fact, no objective, bound "I" exists.

Your notion of a personal self is your sole tie. Therefore, liberation can only happen through liberation from the delusion of a self, existing of itself. Any attempt made on the part of a presumed ego to kill itself would, in any case, only cause the opposite to happen. It would only lead to a stronger attachment and would increase the inner resistance.

Let us now return to Zen Master Huang-po. Elsewhere he says:

> You see the One Mind constantly before you, yet as soon as you begin to reason about it you fall into error.

Why do we constantly see the One Mind before us? It is because everything that you see is the One Mind in the form in which you perceive it. All realms of existence and all states of being are nothing other than manifestations of the Mind.

This gong here, the altar with the buddha statue, this lamp, everything you see is made of the same reality of the One Mind. It is always here! It is always right in front of you in the myriad appearances, in all possible forms.

Mind is not the opposite of matter, but rather it forms matter. It is its substance and thus the sole foundation of all that is material, of all that is form. Form, however, has no reality of its own. That is why Buddhism speaks of shunyata, meaning "void" or "emptiness". Everything is empty. "Form is emptiness, and emptiness is form", says the Mahaprajnaparamita Hridaya

Sutra, the Heart Sutra of Perfection of Great Wisdom. It is the fundamental Sutra which is recited daily in the Zen monasteries.

Form is none other than emptiness, and emptiness shows itself as form. All is one, without a second. Only because of your discriminating perception do you divide everything into the perceiver as subject, the perception process, and the perceived as object. And that makes three. In fact, these three are but one.

All multiplicity is illusion! There is only a single being, the One Mind, beside which nothing else exists. It is the sole reality at the deepest ground of all living beings and of all things. In truth, neither living beings nor objects exist separate from one another. Accordingly, material existence, which means the entire external world of phenomena, is just an illusion and a result of the perceiving consciousness. That is why Huang-po says: "Everything is the One Mind, beside which nothing exists."

Everything you devise or philosophically acquire through rational analysis and conceptual, discriminating thought is mere speculation and has nothing to do with reality. It causes you to fall ever deeper into mental confusion and to distance yourself ever further from the clear light of the Mind which shines behind all experience as the uninvolved observer. This reality, beyond all thinking, is your true being.

Wake up! Stop dreaming, and the original condition of your true being will shine forth in the light of Enlightenment, a hundred thousand times brighter than the sun. In this boundless light, the One Mind reveals itself as the sole existing reality, beside which nothing else exists.

5

At The Moment Of Death

If an ordinary man, when he is about to die, could only see the five elements of existence as void, he would receive Enlightenment in a flash.

ZEN MASTER HUANG-PO (NINTH CENTURY)

This is a wonderful statement by the Chinese Zen Master Huang-po. It is one of the best formulations of Zen teaching there is because, in just a few words, it encompasses what Zen practise is all about.

In Zen you must cast off your wrong understanding and your false viewpoint in order to see through the deceptive nature of all phenomena. Yet by not recognising the emptiness of all phenomena you identify yourself with your old thought models and then believe, "that is the world and that is my personality". That is why all of you who come to me are very weighty personalities – important incarnations. Each of you is something very special.

All your memories, this whole sum of experiences with which you have identified yourself from the first day of your childhood onwards make up your assumed individuality. As it hardens into the armour of the ego, this habitual, identifying way of viewing the world forms the illusion of an independent, self-existing personality. This believes itself to be separate from everything it perceives and experiences.

"I am I and you are you." This is the discriminating, dualistic view of the average samsaric world-fixated person. "I am you and you are me; whoever sees me, sees us; in our self we embrace the universe." This is the multidimensional perspective of the enlightened being. This is the cosmic dimension of the all-encompassing whole, for all assumed multiplicity is in fact an organic, self-contained, all-encompassing whole that contains everything within itself.

"Form is emptiness, and emptiness is form", says the Mahaprajnaparamita Hridaya Sutra, the Heart Sutra of Transcendent Wisdom. Empty means without substance of its own, without being of itself. It is all just phenomena – only form, devoid of all reality.

The entire external world of phenomena has only a relative existence, like for example a mirage, which you cannot say is not there and does not exist. You can actually see the mirage; this wonderful oasis with its refreshing spring and delightful plants. You see it, yet it is no more than a phenomenon, and thus has only a relative reality. In the same way, the whole world has only relative reality. All objects and all phenomena are but illusion.

The external world of phenomena appears to be something it is not, for it is nothing but a gigantic delusion – a delusory notion of the projecting mind.

Everything that can form the contents of your awareness is just a manifestation in your consciousness, without real being. But pure being itself is unconditional being, without dependence on anything that has gone before, and thus having its being out of itself. As the reality of the One Mind, it is the Absolute, it is the suchness of all things – Tathata. It is formless and uncreated since it has its being of itself.

If an ordinary man, when he is about to die ...

The instant of death is a very decisive moment. It is this very moment in which our accustomed and familiar perceptions, the feeling of stability of an external phenomenal world, begins to fade. Everything dissolves away. There is nothing for us to cling to any longer. The entire past, our whole life, is no more than a memory.

Everything merges together to a single point. And this dimension becomes increasingly powerful since no further movement takes place. It is a cut off, a radical end! The thread of life is severed. The pearls of identification on life's string of pearls tumble to the ground, roll away, and disappear.

Enlightened masters of all religions have always maintained that the instant of death is a crucial moment, for as Buddha says: "You will become what you desire." You will be drawn to that on which your heart dwells.

These identifications, whatever they may be, generate the tendencies of the samskaras, the karmic driving forces, which determine your entire earthly existence. Their influence also extends through bardo, the interval state between death and rebirth, and thus determines the form your rebirth will take in the next life.

If, however, at the moment of death you realise the emptiness of this whole deception, of this great ruse, in crystal clear awareness you can pervade all things, and all identifications and attachments will melt away on their own.

The very instant you perceive the "emptiness" of all existence, that is, the emptiness of all apparent existence, in this instance release spontaneously occurs.

You see clearly the deceptive nature of all being and ascend above the dark mists of phenomena into the clear light of reality.

If an ordinary man, when he is about to die, could only see the five elements of existence as void...

This is what it comes down to. So I ask you; why wait so long for it? Why not die the mystical death "now"? Now, in this instant!

The seventeenth century Christian mystic Angelus Silesius says: "Die, ere you die, so that when you die, you will not be ruined."

And Zen Master Ta-hui (twelfth century) says:

> Die while you are still living and be completely dead, then do whatever you want and everything is good!

If you let go now while you still have the power to think clearly and decide for yourselves, if you see through the deception and radically immerse yourselves in here and now, then space and time and hence all else will melt away. The absolute reality behind the whole façade, the empty film screen of the Self Mind, the original condition of your mind, will shine forth with undiminished clarity.

All of a sudden, everything falls away from you – you are completely free and experience the world as though it were for the first time. Huang-po says of this:

> When everything internal and external, physical and spiritual, has been left behind, when, like in the void, no attachment remains behind, when each action is dictated solely by place and circumstance, when subject and object have been forgotten – that is the highest form of letting go.

If you really want to put an end to the circle of birth and death, there is no other way than to let go of everything and free yourself of everything. You must rid yourself of everything that you have ever upheld in your mind and deemed important, for: "Nothing is important in the face of the presence of death!" Yet the smallest hesitation and you could lose life and limb. The Chinese Zen Master Yun-men (tenth century) says of this:

> Time waits for no one: one day your dying gaze will turn to the ground and then, what will you do then? Do not wave your arms and legs around in despair like a crab which has been thrown into hot water! This will definitely not be the place for big words from you big mouths!

"True words are not pleasant, pleasant words are not true", says the Taoist sage Lao-tse. The deeper and more direct a statement is, touching the heart of the matter, the less uplifting are its words in a general sense. They always pull the foundation of your ego's armour out from under it. Everything that gives you ostensible security in this space-time dimension of samsaric delusion all dissolves away.

It is as though you were to find yourself drifting on a sheet of ice in warm waters. The ice is melting away. You can no longer hold on to it. Well you can try, but it will nonetheless melt and return to whence it came.

There are only two choices: either you remain in this deluded state of attachment, which will be your downfall when the pseudo-foundation of an apparently stable external world dissolves, or you are in accord with Tao and let go. When you are in accord with Tao, you move with the flow, you do not try to oppose it. Even when everything melts away, this causes no fear or terror for it means the harmonious homecoming to the original condition of your being. When you realise that the elements of existence forming the delusion of a personality have no being anyway, and all you perceive is no more than an illusion, you will reach a state of inner readiness for detachment from everything.

Everything is the One Mind. There is nothing which is not the One Mind. It is just that the habitual way in which you see things and situations, in terms of attachment and aversion, and well-worn behavioural patterns causes you to smother reality with the delusion of your projections.

It is just like in the evening moonlight, you would see a snake lying across your path. You jump back horrified and run away. The next morning you return and realise – it was only an old rope.

Your conditioned consciousness creates the delusion of a snake, and straight away fear rises in you. You can fabricate everything in your imagination.

It is just like with a potter. The potter has his clay from which he forms all sorts of things. Looking at his display, you see many different-shaped vessels: pitchers, bowls, cups, and all sorts of things, a remarkable assortment of forms. Yet all these different things are nothing but clay, just the same old clay.

The samskaras, your karmic formational forces, form the objects, but the substance, the clay, is the One Mind, beside which nothing exists.

So, my dear friends, why continue to throw pots? Why not abide in the original condition of the Mind? Free yourselves of everything! Be what you truly are, and do not create any new overlay! It is really so simple! The sole cause of your problem is that you have forgotten who you are. If you had not forgotten, you would not have come here.

You come here to ask me "Who am I?" How peculiar indeed. The wave asks the ocean: "Who am I?" And the ocean answers: "You are me!" All of you are the ocean. You yourselves are the reality you seek. Christ says: "The Father and I are one", which means: Whoever sees me, sees us. There is no difference.

Due to its conceptual fixation, thinking leads to differentiation, causing the illusion of multiplicity to arise. Yet where there is multiplicity, there is also separation. You view yourselves apart from the whole, and thus give rise to your myriad problems. In the words of Zen Master Huang-po:

> When thoughts arise, then do all things arise; when thoughts subside, then do all things subside, and with them all problems.

Thinking generates karmic forces and thus mental formations which then activate all emotional impulses and therefore all sorts of mental images. It is just like at night, when you are dreaming. There is no need to dream; nonetheless, memories and undigested impressions of the day begin to act as karmic formational forces. They arise and form themselves into all kinds of situations of enslavement in the circle of birth, ageing, despair, illness, pain, and death.

If you want to put an end to this apparition, you have no other choice than to wake up and thus to die out of the illusion of a projecting consciousness. And this means: Die the mystical death! Master Ta-hui says, "Die while you live! Then do whatever you want; all is good."

Of course, when someone sits here before you and speaks of the necessity of letting go and of mystical death, some of you may start thinking, "This is a gloomy philosophy." But let me tell you, it is neither a gloomy philosophy nor any other kind of philosophy for that matter – it is no philosophy whatsoever – it is the highest truth.

It seems gloomy only to those who cling to the delusion of an independent identity, of the ego-illusion. If you cling to it you will naturally have a very hard time letting go of it, just like a child who has built a sand castle and someone comes along and kicks it in. What a pity! But why take autumn leaves for gold? Why shed tears over something that is nothing more than an illusion and has no true being anyway?

Only those fight against thoughts on the inevitability of having to die who are already spiritually dead anyway. That is why Christ says: "Let the dead bury their own and follow me!" Yet following the truth means accepting death and immersing yourself in it completely. In his wonderful poem "The Great Death", Soji Enku says: "The great death, your life bows over you with a smile. Welcome it with all the roses of love."

That is it. That is the truth. In the moment when you forget, having forgotten yourself and all things, and you surrender yourself completely to death, you will be granted the "Great Life" and you will shout out: "How wonderful!

There is no birth and there is no death, and there is no highest truth to reach." There is no imprisonment in the circle of birth and death and there is no liberation.

Everything is MU! That is the way it is. MU – nothing! You must become this nothing – completely be it. But do not cling to the word MU, or else you will be stuck again. Be sure it does not happen to you as it did to the monk in the following example:

> A Zen monk goes to Zen Master Joshu and says, "Look, Master, I have cast away everything. What do you say to that?" To illustrate his point, he waves his sleeves demonstratively.
> Old Master Joshu looks at the monk in a bored way and says: "Very well then, throw it away." The monk, obviously confused by Joshu's reply, thinks the master has not understood him due to his old age and says, "But Master, I just told you I have let go of everything. What is left for me to throw away?"
> Joshu replies, "Oh, in that case you will have to continue to carry it."

The monk truly believed he had achieved MU and let go, but old Joshu immediately recognised that the disciple was just clinging tightly to his notion of having let go. The disciple's MU was nothing more than a thought construction and not the true MU of Zen. But what is the true MU of Zen? Die and be completely dead! Then do whatever you want and everything is good, just as it is. In other words:

> Hanging at the edge of the abyss, let go of everything and die completely, then return to life – then nothing can deceive you anymore.

This mystical death is to plunge into the "Great Life". The Great Death and the Great Life are one and the same. Letting go completely and dissolving into the plenitude of the divine being is "one" experience which takes place at one single moment.

Leave everything behind you! Stop grasping for the ungraspable. Then your true face before your birth will shine forth, a thousand times brighter than the sun, and you will be filled with great clarity and indescribable peace.

That is "the Freedom of Zen". The bonds of ego-delusion are broken, and you live a life of complete freedom in the midst of the world.

6

True Zen Practise

The void needs no support, it relies upon nothing. Without effort, remaining relaxed and natural, you can break the yoke and gain liberation.
If you see nothing when you look into space, and simultaneously the mind perceives the Mind, you destroy all discrimination and attain buddhahood.
The clouds that wander through the sky have no roots, no abode; just like the discriminating thoughts that float through the mind. Once the Self-Mind is seen, discrimination stops.

Tilopa (eleventh century)

"The void needs no support, it relies upon nothing." The boundless expanse of the One Mind needs no support; it relies upon nothing. It is as vast and as open as the boundless sky, without hindrance or bounds. All systems of thought and all the contrived philosophies and religions ever fabricated are entirely the consequence of acrobatic cerebral speculation, and thus constantly need new crutches, scaffolds, and mental props to keep them from falling in on themselves. Zen Master Huang-po says, "You cannot nail a board to the void." Reality itself is inexpressible; it relies on nothing at all. Everything we could say of it would fall short of the mark.

Without effort, remaining relaxed and natural ...

Many people are of the opinion that Zen is a very

difficult undertaking, and in certain Zen books too you are repeatedly told how exceedingly difficult Zen is. Some western authors even write that Westerners will never be fully able to reach a deeper understanding of Zen anyway.

People always make such a mystery out of Zen, but let me tell you, Zen is not difficult, it is in fact very simple. We could call it a "difficult simplicity". The difficulty in understanding Zen lies solely in not understanding how close you are to the reality you seek. That is the crux of the matter. And because it is so close that it cannot be any closer, there is truly nothing to seek.

"That there is nothing to achieve are not empty words but the highest truth", says Huang-po – as evident as these words may sound, only very few people understand them. Although you quickly agree and say, "there is nothing to achieve", intellectually speaking you remain goal-oriented, and you keep this up, regardless of what you do – even during meditation.

Most people use mediation in order to achieve something. They wish to attain a pleasant, uplifting feeling. They wish to abide in quietude and peace. True Zen meditation, however, means being free from every desire, whatever it may be. In Zen we have the expression "mushotoku" for this, which means, "without desire for gain or profit".

If you cling to pleasant, uplifting feelings, inevitably the moment will come where these feelings change and take on a new direction. They transform into opposite feelings and you fall into a sad state.

This quietist meditation form of enrapturing feelings is like a drug. It can become an addiction. Yet each time when the pleasant feelings change and turn about, you start to suffer. You experience a little happiness, but then you fall into the opposite state, becoming more and more trapped in your self-made world of opposites. If you cling to this false form of meditation, you will never be able to fulfil your original, true being. It cannot liberate you from your entrapment in birth and death.

Whenever I think of this enrapturing meditation, I am reminded of the following situation I experienced: On the fourth day of my first Zen sesshin with my Master Soji Enku I started to have such knee pains that my meditation posture became very unpleasant. I stole a glance at my neighbour to my right, but he was sitting on his meditation cushion with a perfect posture and a wide, cheerful smile over his whole face. "Oh, how good it would be", I thought, "if I too could meditate in such a joyful way."

Suddenly, the Master was standing behind my neighbour and started hitting him with his stick. "Wake up", he roared, "come out of your devil's cave of pleasant feelings!" "Oh", I thought, "how good it is that I don't have such a joyful meditation."

Just as it is wrong to bathe in enrapturing feelings during meditation, it is equally wrong to just sit around, drifting off as mindless as cattle. How can you ever expect to achieve insight into your true being by just mindlessly sitting around?

When Ma-tsu was still a disciple of his Master Nan-yueh (eighth century), he had to recognise this too.

> At the time when Ma-tsu was still a disciple in the monastery of his Master Nan-yueh, he sat

day in, day out for many hours at a time in meditation. One day, when he was sitting immersed in the monastery yard, his master came up to him and asked, "What are you hoping to achieve by sitting absorbed for hours on end?" Ma-tsu replied, "I wish to gain Buddhahood this way."

Without uttering a word, Nan-yueh turned around and went into the garden. After a while he returned with a stone and a roof tile and began to grate the stone against the tile. Young Ma-tsu's sacred peace and tranquility were shattered by the grinding noise. He strove to ignore the terrible noise but Master Nan-yueh continued unremittingly to grate the stone against the tile. Finally, having put up with the ordeal for several minutes, Ma-tsu could no longer contain himself and called out irascibly, "Master, why do you continue to grind this stone and the tile together?" Nan-yueh replied: "I plan to make a mirror out of the tile." Totally baffled, Ma-tsu then asked, "But how can you make a mirror by grinding a roof tile?" To this Master Nan-yueh answered, "How can anyone reach Buddhahood by sitting in contemplation?"

In this way, Master Nan-yueh wanted to make it clear to his student that Buddhahood – experiencing your true being – cannot be forced by external, artificially imposed practise. The ancient Chinese Zen masters called this false form of meditation practise "the ghost cave of the dead void". Zen Master Fo-yan (twelfth century) says:

> True Zen meditation does not mean that you just sit there and take no notice of anything. Do not practise by sitting bolt-upright, suppressing mind and body and turning them into earth and wood – this yields nothing.

Nowadays, there are many Zen monks who simply just sit there and snooze. But how can they ever expect to achieve insight into their true being by just mindlessly sitting around.

The vital Zen practise of original Zen is altogether different from mere sitting in the quietude of inner silence. Zen meditation practise is – and I cannot stress this enough – absolutely necessary if you want to achieve realisation of your true self.

Nevertheless, it would be a great mistake to believe that the only aim in Zen is to realise stillness of mind. That is why we do not practise the bone-breaking Japanese kamikaze form of zazen, where all you do is sit on your meditation cushion and stare at the wall.

Many Japanese monasteries hold Zen sesshins where all you do is perch on your meditation cushion for days or even weeks on end and just sit and sit and sit. You are even "generously" allowed to nod off for an hour after midnight on your cushion – provided, of course, you maintain an upright position. Zen Master Lin-chi has the following to say about this type of false practise:

> There are the blind bald-headed ones who, after they have stuffed themselves full, practise zazen for hours on end. They arrest the movement of their thoughts and to prevent them from even forming, they flee the noise of the world and

seek quietude. This is a deviant form of Zen. It is the pitfall of the dead void.

This dead form of zazen is the exact opposite of the Zen of the ancient Chinese masters. Most people are convinced that the only true form of Zen meditation is to sit with a bolt-upright posture and crossed legs. But the truth of it is that meditation in sitting is, taken by itself, not complete meditation practise. Whoever clings to meditation in sitting as the sole, correct form, is clinging one-sidedly to the physical aspect of sitting.

True Zen meditation does not require you to retain a prescribed posture for long periods. Zazen does not mean to sit stiff as a corpse. "Za" means to sit in the sense of to abide. "Zen" means to be immersed in reality itself, the source of our being. That is the point – to abide in this state of immersion.

Emphasis should not be placed on a physical viewpoint but rather on the attitude of "Mind" from one moment to the next in everything that you do. Whether standing, lying down, sitting, walking, talking, being silent – everywhere and at all times, without interruption. This is the original, living Zen of the ancient Chinese masters, and everything else is the abnormal outgrowth of overstrained brains. The Chinese Zen Master Hui-jang says:

> Whoever practises meditation in sitting tries to become a sitting buddha. When you practise zazen, you should be aware that true Zen is neither in sitting or in lying. If you train yourself to become a sitting buddha, you should be aware that buddha has no fixed form. Trying to make yourself become a sitting buddha is just like

killing buddha. Whoever clings to the sitting form will never reach the deep truth of Zen.

Hui-neng, the sixth patriarch of Zen, who lived in China in the eighth century, expresses it with the following words:

A living one, who sits and does not lie.
A dead one, who lies and does not sit.
In the end, they are all but filthy skeletons!

Persisting in one-sided sitting meditation reveals a narrow-minded, dogmatic clinging to a particular notion of Zen. But as long as you still have a single notion of Zen, it no longer is true Zen.

Original Zen, as was taught and lived by the Chinese masters of old, is a very powerful and vivacious Zen which rises above all forms of discrimination. And assuming non-discrimination is a major element in Zen, a true man of Zen will not withdraw himself for the rest of his life in a monastery and sit on his meditation cushion with folded legs staring at the wall, and take this to be true, real Zen practise. Much more, he will perceive that it is all about achieving a non-discriminating clarity of mind within this multitudinous world of discrimination.

In Zen practice, you aim to retain a state of mind free from attachments, everywhere and constantly, so that you learn to deal with things in a non-identifying free way. So that you learn to possess things without them possessing you. So that you act without ego-relatedness; so that you are inwardly free of your actions. This is true life, out of, through, and in Zen.

"When it is necessary to act, then act – when the necessity is over, then be still", says Huang-po.

> A Zen student asks his master:
> "Master, what is your way of living Zen – what is the secret of your Zen?"
> The master replies: "When I am hungry, I eat, and when I am tired, I sleep."
> "Yes", says the monk, "that is all very well, but we all do that. What is so special about it?"
> "Well", says the master, "when you eat, your head is full of thoughts and you are scattered here and there, and when you sleep, your dreams are filled with fears and desires. But when I eat, I eat and nothing else. And when I sleep, I sleep and nothing else. That is my Zen."

Without effort, remaining relaxed and natural ...

This is true zazen and at the same time, the attitude of mind of Taoism. We should not forget that the ancient Chinese Zen masters such as Hui-neng, Ma-tsu, Pai-chang, Huang-po, Lin-chi were steeped in the spirit of Tao. However, the essential element of Taoism is wu-wei, nondoing, the relaxed and easeful attitude of mind of nondesire. Tao flows like water, and when you are in accordance with Tao, you are in harmonic unison with the all-embracing wholeness of Being.

Therefore, do not create any barriers or artificial pathways! Do not fetter yourselves with dogmatic chains, and do not wall yourselves into the dungeon of any system! That is not in accordance with the spirit of Tao and the original, true spirit of Chan (the Chinese word for Zen).

To avoid confusion, and to guard against anyone thinking we practise the bone-breaking Japanese form of Zen here, we call our centre the Tao Chan Zen Centre.

"Tao Chan" is composed of the Chinese terms Tao and Chan, and stands for spiritual practise in the midst of the world. Tao means the Absolute, and at the same time the Way. Chan, the Chinese word for Zen, means immersion. Tao Chan is therefore the connection between Way and immersion, whereby the active way of everyday life connects to the crystal-clear self-awareness of the mind in silent Zen meditation.

Without effort, remaining relaxed and natural, you can break the yoke and gain liberation.

"Ha!" one of you may say, "Now I have him. He has just given himself away: breaking the yoke is yet again a forceful act." – No! It is not forceful.

The moment you effortlessly abide in a relaxed and natural state there is no longer any ego fixation or artificial behaviour. There only remains the spirit of wu-wei, nondoing, and wu-nien, nonthinking.

This is the true spirit of Zen. In this state of cheerful reflection of the Mind, your attachment and identification, desire, hate, and ignorance fade away. The same goes for age, despair, sickness, pain, and death; they all disappear and you abide in the all-embracing entireness of Being. Not that you will never grow any older and die, but it will just happen.

Things take their natural course. The plant grows, the bud opens, becomes a flower and blooms in full splendour and beauty. The flower gives off its wonderful scent, attracting bees and butterflies to take its nectar, and then comes the time when it loses its petals and falls apart. Everything happens quite naturally, in harmony with Tao.

If you see nothing when you look into space, and simultaneously the mind perceives the Mind, you destroy all discrimination and attain buddhahood.

"If you see nothing when you look into space" means: Things are still there when you look into space while abiding in the cheerful reflection of the Mind, but you no longer view a dualistic world of discrimination of subject and object.

No longer do you, as ego-centred subject, perceive external objects in the discriminating light of good and evil, right and wrong, desire and rejection. Much rather, everything is an all-encompassing organic whole which includes everything within itself, in a wonderful and perfect way. You look outward, but because your perception is no longer dualistic, your outward-looking is non-outward-looking. There is neither outside nor inside, all that remains is pure "suchness" – Tathata. Everything is just as it is.

Everything is the One Mind, beside which nothing exists. The seer, the seen, and the process of seeing: all of this is one. The thinker, the thoughts, and the process of thinking fall together into one, and multiplicity melts away.

Neither the object of perception nor the perceiver or thinker has any reality of its own. A thinker as subject does not exist. The thinker is nothing more than an accumulation of impressions, collected since birth. Everything is merely occurrence! It is all just a psychic process! All that exists is a sequence of thoughts, based on existing concepts.

When I say there is no thinker as subject, many people become afraid. But such fears are totally ungrounded and merely betray attachment to something that does not exist. When you truly leave everything just as it is and allow yourself to become completely immersed in this suchness, in here and now, the phantasm will disappear and there will be no more differentiation. Then everything is good just as it is. Then, the reality behind the phenomena will reveal itself.

The same goes for the cinema screen behind the images. The projections of an external multitudinous phenomenal world, caused by the process of attachment and aversion, will cease. The film of birth, ageing, despair, illness, pain, and death is over and the clear light of reality shines forth. In this instant, it is as Meister Eckhart says, "The eye with which you see God, and the eye with which God sees you is one eye, one seeing and one perceiving". Tilopa says of this:

If you see nothing when you look into space, and simultaneously the mind perceives the Mind, you destroy all discrimination and attain buddhahood.

However, attainment cannot be compared to climbing a mountain, for example. It is not some distant goal that you eventually achieve. Instead, it is always present as your innermost true being.

Christ says: "The kingdom of God is within you", as translated by Luther. Other translations read: "The kingdom of God is among you." And yet the two translations do not contradict each other, contrary to what many highbrow theologians think but rather, they complement one another.

Theologians are very divided here, and argue over which of the translations is the correct one, "within you" or "among you", but the crux of it is that both are equally correct. One complements the other. The reality of all-encompassing being, the reality of the One Mind, is within you and simultaneously, constantly present everywhere as your innate reality. The Chinese Zen masters say: "Look beneath the soles of your feet, there you will find Tao, there you will find reality."

> *The clouds that wander through the sky have no roots, no abode; just like the discriminating thoughts that float through the mind. Once the Self-Mind is seen, discrimination stops.*

Your thoughts and visions that cross the Self-Mind have no reality, no stability; they simply pass by. They are like passing clouds which can do no other than to disperse at some point in time.

Just like the evening clouds that pass before the moon, the clouds of your discriminating thoughts pass before the Self-Mind. And thus it can happen that, in the evening, you look up to a cloudy sky, and seeing no moon say: "There is no moon tonight." But the moon is always there, just as is the self-illuminating Self-Mind, only you are not there, and that is the whole problem. It always shines, it is always present, even when it is hidden behind the dark clouds of discriminating, conceptual thought. Yet as soon as the Self-Mind is seen, all discrimination ends and you awaken from your dream of a three-dimensional external world, and you are free.

7

There Is Nothing To Achieve

Our original buddha-nature is, in highest truth, devoid of any atom of objectivity. It is void, omnipresent, silent, and pure. It is glorious and mysterious peaceful joy – and that is all.

ZEN MASTER HUANG-PO (NINTH CENTURY)

Our original buddha-nature is our original, true being, beyond birth and death. This true original condition of the Mind, as seen from the standpoint of the highest truth, is devoid of any perceptible attribute. It eludes all denomination. It is true being, in which all is contained – an all-pervading, unending universal consciousness, and the origin of all things. Zen Buddhists call it: "Our original countenance before our birth". Zen Master Huang-po says:

It is void, omnipresent, silent, and pure.

"Void" refers to shunyata, in the sense that whatever we could say of our original true being has nothing to do with the thing itself. It is a reality above being, without attributes, which lies beyond the realm of intellectual recognition. As the fullness of the divine void, it is the beyond-being nonbeing; omnipresent, silent, and pure. Since it is omnipresent, it is "now-here" and thus you do not need to seek it. There is nothing to achieve, since there is also nothing to seek. All your seeking in this and that and here and there takes place solely due to your spiritual blindness and your ignorance. It arises from the erroneous belief that absolute reality is something you can achieve by means of various external, artificial activities. However much effort you put into it you will not achieve Truth in this way. In fact, the more you try, the more you distance yourself from it. This is the great dilemma.

All religions and philosophies say you need to do this and that, practise asceticism, study philosophical works and commentaries, practise meditation for hours on end and so forth.

Many spiritual seekers use these and other methods to strive towards realisation. Most of them become so enamoured by one of their methods that it becomes a means to an end, and thus a great hurdle on the path to liberation.

Zen has nothing to do with all these artificial methods. It points unequivocally to your original condition of being – directly and immediately. This is where "the Freedom of Zen" is revealed. And so: leave everything behind you, free yourself of everything, whatever it may be!

In the eyes of the ancient Zen masters, all Buddhist teachings, as expounded in the sutras and shastras, are nothing more than worthless toilet paper, there to wipe up the intellect's refuse. Zen has nothing to do with philosophical quibblings and logical reasoning. That is why Zen rejects everything that has even the slightest inkling of an external teaching. It fosters absolute trust in a person's inner being. In Zen, all truth comes from within.

Zen has nothing to do with any fixed religious dogma, whatever it may be. As such, it has absolutely no interest in the empty fantasy products of theological speculative erudition. Zen is not a product of discriminating, conceptual thought, but rather, its main aim is to free you from your intellectual prison.

The development of intuitive comprehension, instead of intellectual study, is always the fundamental aspect of Zen practise. The main features of Zen were summarised during the early Tang-dynasty into four tenets:

1. Transmission outside orthodox teaching
2. Independence from sacred texts
3. Directly pointing to the Mind (Hsin)
4. Perceiving one's own nature and achieving Buddhahood

The reality you seek only reveals itself when you recognise that there is nothing at all for you to seek. All seeking is out of ignorance. Not seeking means remaining at ease. Zen Master Fo-yan says of this:

> When you seek, what difference is there to chasing after sound and form?
> When you do not seek, then what is the difference between you and earth, wood, and stone?
> You must seek without seeking!

This means: become silent, abide in yourself, and thus let yourself be found by the all-embracing, all-present reality of the One Mind. Meister Eckhart puts it so: "A person does not have to ask for the grace of God. He must simply hold himself in readiness for it."

Remember the parable of the man who stands at the gates of paradise and tries to enter. At first, he knocks tentatively, then a little harder, but nothing happens.

Then he pounds with his fist, but without success. Despairingly, he kicks the gates, then, with a run up, he runs against the gates, all without success.

He continues his attempts throughout the night until at last he collapses to the ground, realising that all his attempts were in vain. Yet lo and behold, the gates open, but in the opposite direction – towards him. That is it! All of your seeking and all your efforts to reach the unreachable do nothing other than to push shut the gates to liberation. The Chinese Zen Master Yuan-wu points to the futility of seeking with the following words:

> If you wish to experience Zen directly, above all do not seek it. What is attained by seeking has already been soiled by your thinking. Only when you stop your compulsive thinking, to reach the point where all things are unborn, do you break through to freedom. You no longer fall into feelings and you do not dwell on concepts. Instead, you transcend everything well and truly.
> Then the presence of Zen is crystal clear everywhere in the world, with the totality of everything transforming into ultimate completeness.
> Everything originates from your own heart. This is what those of old called "retrieving the family treasure".

"There is nothing to attain" is one of the most important basic principles in Zen – in fact it is the quintessential statement of Zen. "That there is nothing to be reached are not empty words but the highest truth." How often did I hear Huang-po's words uttered from the mouth of my Master Soji Enku. Over and over again he said: "My dear young friend, believe me, there is really nothing to achieve, there is no Enlightenment to reach." The more you live in the illusion that there is something to be gained or something to achieve, the more you distance yourself from your true being.

What is it you want to gain? There are no new possessions to acquire. Everything is present, here and now! The truth of Zen reveals itself "right here", in this instant. It is neither in the past nor in the future.

Here and Now is eternity itself; space and time are no more than a result of thinking, and thus illusion. "Right now", in this instant, be truly "here", without thoughts, concepts, or visions! Immerse yourself completely in this moment. This is the instantaneous way to directly perceiving reality as it is.

Following the Zen way means immersing yourself in the truth of Here-Now. Since the truth is the all-embracing totality of being, it embraces boundless space and all three notions of time; past, present, and future in a single Now.

Now-here, everything falls into one single point. In the words of the Tantra Master Saraha (ninth century): "Everything that is here is elsewhere too, and whatever is not here is nowhere."

Where do you hope to gain an inch of land when you are already standing right in the middle of it? Where would you seek the "Pure Land" of Sukhavati Paradise of buddha Amitabha?

The ancient Chinese masters said: "If you seek Tao, then look beneath the soles of your feet!"

Let me remind you of the passage in the Bible where the Pharisees come to ask Jesus, "You talk the whole time about the kingdom of God. You say the kingdom of God is nigh at hand. But just how close is it and how will we recognise it when it comes, and how and when will it come?" And Jesus replies:

> Amen, I say to you: The kingdom of God cometh not that you see it with external signs. Neither shall you say: Lo it is here, or it is there – for Amen I say to you, the Kingdom of God is within you!

When Jesus says, "the kingdom of God is within you", this "within" is the core of all being. It is your innermost self, the place and origin of all life. It is the cave of divine darkness, the "krypta of the heart", as the Christian mystics say. This is where the light of our true nature shines. Like the sun, it lights up the entire universe and reveals itself to us when we perceive that which is concealed.

This temple of the Holy Spirit is the "Guha Hridaya"; the cave of the heart of the Upanishads, which, as man's innermost sanctum, contains the unborn divine light. In the Chandogya Upanishad it is written:

> This light which shines above the heavens, above all the worlds, beyond everything, higher than the highest worlds, is the same light which shines within man.

This is the Kingdom of God, your true being "within you". And because this innermost self is beyond both birth and death and space and time, it can be nothing other than "Now". The innermost self can never be the past or the future. Such are merely clouds that pass in front of the clear light of the Mind and have no substance. Behind them, reality shines with undiminishing clarity – eternal, unborn, indestructible, and beyond the bounds of space and time.

Since this is so, and the reality of the One Mind manifests itself as the foundation of all you experience, it is thus "among you". Do you seek the Kingdom of God? It is right beneath you; you are standing on it. Look beneath the soles of your feet!

Wherever you go, wherever you stand, wherever you are, the unchanging buddha-essence, the original source of the entire cosmos, is present. So why do you jump restlessly from branch to branch like wild monkeys, grasping at this and that and searching for something that you have in fact never lost? What madness!

It is glorious and mysterious peaceful joy – and that is all.

How will you be able to find this true joy? You will only find it when you immerse yourself in the original condition of the Mind, your true being "now-here." This, your original true self, is in fact none other than "glorious and mysterious peaceful joy."

But if you go about with the cramped demeanour of a pallbearer, convinced of being able to obtain great joy through conceptual thought and your notions of acceptance and rejection, of right and wrong, you are on the wrong track. As long as you continue clinging to duality and maintain the belief of thus being able to gain access to mysterious peaceful joy, to experience great divine joy, you are trapped in dualistic thought – you are a prisoner of your intellect. The intellect constantly tries to attach and set limits since it can keep control of what is limited and thus avoid opening itself and letting go. But as long as you cling to your conditioning and the interwoven memories of your dead past, refusing to open yourself, you will never experience true joy. On the contrary: when divine joy catches sight of you it will hastily take flight.

A sombre person who skulks through life with a face like a pallbearer can never become enlightened. Sombreness is a totally misguided attitude to life.

The Vedanta Master Shankara (ninth century) says, "You are Brahman, pure consciousness, the observer behind every experience and your true essence is joy." But cramped sombreness is simply foul and pathological. It is a destructive illness, a cancer of the soul.

A humourless, sombre attitude of mind is always the result of conditioned, ego-embroiled problem-thinking. Fearfully you peer into the future, and filled with melancholy or a guilty conscience you look back into the past. This fear is the reason for mistrust, jealousy, and envy, making the "I" into a fortress against everything that surrounds it. This disquiets your heart and scatters your mind.

You wear protective armour because you are afraid of being vulnerable and thus you defend yourself against everything and everyone. Subsequently, you more and more lose the ability to perceive your true being behind all the unrestrained projections of your dualistic consciousness. Eventually, your existence, separated from reality, becomes no more than a tawdry shadow of your true being. As such you become a walking corpse. Now that you no longer take heed of the harmonic tone of life, you can only perceive disharmony in the world.

Just as a mirror only ever reflects back the face that looks into it, so the perceived world only ever reflects your state of consciousness. It is like in the old Tibetan parable of the dog in the hall of mirrors:

One day, while roaming around, a dog once became lost in a cave with many passages. He suddenly finds himself in a big hall, surrounded by a thousand mirrors. Wherever he looks he sees only dogs, nothing but dogs. Frightened and distrustful, he bristles and backs away a few steps. Since the dogs in the thousand mirrors do the same, he begins to growl, snarl, and bare his teeth ferociously. Growing terrified at the huge number of ferocious dogs he sees all around him, he falls into a state of utter confusion. He begins to run angrily in circles, which, of course, the dogs in the mirrors do as well. This causes him to run faster and faster until all at once, he falls down dead.

Now comes the question: What would have happened had the poor dog just once wagged his tail? And so my dear friends, stop your growling and wag your tails instead.

An Indian proverb says, "The smile that you send out will return to you." The world is just a reflection of your self, and there is no sense in finding fault in a reflection.

We cannot change the reflected image of the world. If we want to live in a joyful and peaceful world we must begin with ourselves; this is an irrefutable spiritual law.

However, the prerequisite for inner readiness to open your heart to all beings is selfless concern and compassionate love for all living beings. However, only by overcoming your own conditioning can this take place so that you surpass the world of opposites and experience the consubstantiality of all beings. This is the only way for you to find peace within yourself and plant love, tolerance, and peace in the world.

I have often said: As long as you do not truly live and truly breathe the joy of being, totally experiencing and feeling it in every pore of your body, you will remain caught in illusion. And by joy, I am not talking about external joy you only feel when things are going your way, when, for example, you are lying in bed with a beautiful woman, or you find yourself in a wonderful landscape, or a delightful meal is before you and you say: "Oh, how marvellous. What a wonderful world it is." – No!

"Every" day is a good day, says Zen. Regardless of where you are, wherever it may be. Everywhere and constantly, the fullness of divine being manifests itself. This means that the joy of being is constantly present, it is always there – but you are not there.

When you let go of all those things in your head you consider important, what you believe you are, and what you think belongs to you, you will abide in the boundless joy of being.

But since you cling to a plethora of triflings, you constantly produce a multitude of attachments. Diverse notions and all kinds of opinions arise. As a result, you become ensnared in the chains of your conditioning and are no longer able to see anything wrong in what you love, and anything good in what you dislike. Eventually, all sorts of preferences and fears are born.

Take my advice, "leave everything just as it is, whatever it may be." When you let everything take its natural course, you will live in unison with the world. Do not project your moral attitudes, conceptual fixations, behavioural patterns, and your entire conditioning onto everything you see. Instead, let everything flow of its own accord.

Flow along with it! You walk through town and pass a pretty woman who smiles at you. Or you come across a teetering drunk who gabbles and swears at you. Everything is good just as it is, for all is the one ocean of being. One wave is somewhat rounder, the other a little more pointed, another has a foam crest, and another has more bubbles. Yet everything is the one ocean. Everything is perfect.

Be one with the all-embracing entirety of being. Do not fixate, do not label, do not judge, but abide in the original condition of the Mind. Stop dreaming and awaken! To be awake is to be free of all conditioning. This freedom is not meant in the sense of external liberation from things, but as liberation from your false viewpoint and the way in which you attach to things. Zen Master Huang-po says:

> The ignorant eschew the external world but not the thoughts on the world; the wise eschew thoughts on the external world but not the world.

As long as you still try to free yourself of things and of your attachment to them, you will only go round in circles like a dog with a stumped tail trying to bite itself in this stump. Round and round the dog goes, without success. However much you try to free yourself from things in this way, you will never transcend birth and death.

Zen is a radical break in your whole spiritual life, or better, in what is commonly mistaken for spiritual life. Strictly speaking, it is no true spiritual life at all, but in general terms, is deemed as being a spiritual life.

In this form and that form you toil away, studying religious and philosophical texts, and so forth. Yet in truth, these are all but corpses, devoid of all life. Beliefs, dogmas, philosophy, and theology, all of them just corpses. You squander your life on pointless exertion and end up sinking deeper and deeper into the sea of suffering of birth and death.

All of you are walking on mental crutches. Since you are afraid of walking without help, you prop yourselves up with all sorts of madness. But Zen calls out for you to throw away your crutches.

Zen takes the sword of "non-discriminating realisation" and slices through the Gordian knot of your spiritual confusion. The entire delusionary structure falls to pieces and the endless expanse of the One Mind shines forth. Indeed, this is exactly what makes Zen different from all other religious systems and philosophical teachings. To remove a tree, Zen does not start by clipping the smallest leaves, one leaf at a time, then moving down to clip the twigs one after the other, until it reaches the bottom. Even before reaching the bottom, new shoots have started to grow at the top, and thus the whole process starts all over again. This is not the way of Zen.

With the sword of realisation Zen fells the whole tree in a single stroke. Whack! The whole delusionary structure is cut at the roots. That is it! That is the true Zen way, the way of total liberation. In the words of Zen-Master Huang-po:

The mind is filled with radiant clarity, so cast off the darkness of your old, dead concepts. Free yourself of everything!

Now you might be thinking: "Where do I begin with this total liberation? Maybe I should start with my car. I really don't need such a large one, a smaller car would do just as well." Then you begin to tackle one area after the other, but this is exactly the false principle which I have just been talking about.

This is no different from trying to fell a tree by starting clipping the leaves at the very top. The only real way you can remove this whole problem is by discarding yourselves, so that the causing factor is eliminated. And the causing factor is the "ego", the end-product of the three kleshas, the three basic errors: greed, hatred, and blindness, which stand for desire, aggression, and ignorance. The three kleshas interact to create the delusion of an independently existing personality, which amounts to no more than an illusion, lacking any reality whatsoever.

How long do you want to continue playing this game? Why not awaken? – Now! The best opportunity is right now. There is no other and no better opportunity than "Now".

The great Zen way is nothing for the small-minded. Why wait? Why say: "The Master gave another good talk today. I think I am starting to catch on. Some things seem a little clearer, and someday ..."

Forget someday! There is no someday. Past and future are just thoughts that appear in the mind in the present moment. The experience of time is thus nothing else than thinking, and "all thought is an erroneous belief", and therefore nonexistent. There is only "Now" and nothing else. Right now, in this instant, your original face reveals itself – nothing could be closer. Immerse yourself in it now! There is no other way.

In Zen, personal experience is everything. There is no other way than to awaken to your true being. Awaken! Stop dreaming and playing around in the sandbox of your conditionings. Cease viewing things through the template of your conceptual fixations, your social ideals and moral attitudes, and judging what is good and what is not good, what is right and what is wrong! There will be no end if you continue this way. Zen can never be made the object of logical explanations. The ancient Chinese Zen Masters made this clear to their disciples in a distinctive way:

> Master Yun-men entered the dharma hall and said, "Is there anyone here who is able to ask me a question? Well, come on, ask me!"
> A monk stepped forward, bowed, and said, "Please test me, master!"
> The master said, "I cast out a line to catch a giant fish. But what do I have here? A frog!"
> The monk said, "Do not be deceived, master!"
> The master replied to this, "Do you not think you have bitten off more than you can chew?"
> The monk did not know what to say.
> The master beat him with his stick.

Do not deceive yourself by trusting intellectual knowledge. Do not seek at this place and at that place for the truth. All you must do is abstain from discriminating, conceptual thought, so leave everything just as it is and everything is good! This is the way to instantaneously realising the truth.

Zen calls upon you to leave everything just as it is. And to this end, there is nothing for you to do. Zen is a matter of leaving be, not doing. That is it! Let everything go, free yourself of everything, whatever it may be, and the reality of your true being will manifest itself. That which is constantly before you each instant is the boundless One Mind in all its perfection.

It is of the utmost importance that you experience this ubiquitous One Mind, which pervades everything with its piercing brightness. It is the sole reality; there is nothing besides it. This Mind, which has no beginning, is unborn and indestructible. Huang-po has the following to say on the reality of the One Mind:

> This pure Mind, the source of everything, shines forever and on all with the brilliance of its own perfection. But the people of the world do not awake to it, regarding only that which sees, hears, feels and knows as mind. Blinded by their own sight, hearing, feeling and knowing, they do not perceive the spiritual brilliance of the source-substance. If they would finally throw off all conceptual thought in a flash this source-substance would manifest itself like the sun ascending through the void and illuminating the whole universe without hindrance or bounds.

Everything without exception – all living beings and all things – are this buddha-essence in the manifestation of how it appears to the reflecting, perceiving consciousness. For "everything is the One Mind, beside which nothing exists". But ignorance and your spiritual blindness produce an endless multitude of thought waves on the self-existing reality of the One Mind. These waves are the manifold forms in an apparent external phenomenal world that you take for reality and become entangled in. Thus you fail to realise that the world you perceive is your own projection, caused by your discriminating consciousness of accepting and rejecting. Therefore, the world you experience is perceived solely due to duality.

Absolutely everything you encounter is in truth the One Mind in all its perfection. There is nothing besides it! It includes the pretty woman who passes you on the street and smiles at you. It includes the tottering drunk who bawls and swears at you.

Everything is the all-embracing reality of divine being in its completeness. And everything imperfect, or rather what you perceive as imperfect, is simply your own projection.

You put your projected values over the object of your perception and take them for the object itself. But that is a mistake.

For as long as you live in the dream of samsara, in the dream of maya, all you perceive is your own projection, and thus mere appearance, devoid of being. Being is that which obtains its being of itself — there is no beginning, there is no end. There is neither birth nor ageing, nor despair, illness, pain, and death. There is only "that which cannot be expressed". "MU – nothing!" and not a thing besides. All else, whatever it may be, is your own projection. All discrimination in terms of good and bad, sacred and profane is a result of your ignorance. "Vast emptiness, nothing sacred." This is the answer Emperor Wu from Liang received from Bodhidharma as he was asked, "What is the most sacred in the world?" This reminds me of a good mondo with Zen Master Joshu:

> A monk asked, "What does it mean 'to be holy'?"
> Joshu replied, "To sink a mountain of shit into a clear plane."
> Completely bewildered, the monk then begged, "Master, please explain this."
> Joshu cried: "Stop fucking my brain."

Stop projecting, and free yourself from your habitual restricted, dualistic view. The Inexpressible, which is beyond all words and all discrimination is your original face before your birth.

You must leave everything behind you: Buddha, Enlightenment, dharma, Zen, whatever it may be. All of these are merely empty word-shells, and of no use whatsoever. As long as you still cling to words, you can never directly experience your true being.

> Once, a Zen monk asked his master, "Can you point me the way without using words?"
> The master replied to this, "Ask me, without using words."

Zen requires you to negate absolutely everything, then transcend even this negation too. For as long as you still have the smallest trace of negation or affirmation in you, you are still a thousand miles apart from the truth of Zen. Whoever opens his mouth to affirm or negate is lost. He is apart from Zen. To this, Zen Master Bassui (fourteenth century) says:

> Whatever you say is wrong. And if you say nothing, it is equally wrong.

In one of his elucidations, Zen Master I-tuan said:

> "Speech is blasphemy, silence misleading. Above speech and silence there is a way out, but my mouth is not wide enough to point you to it." With these words he arose from his high chair and departed.

In here and now, radically let go and immerse yourself in the original condition of the Mind. That is all there is to it. When you have achieved complete realisation, you will experience no other than this omnipresent buddha-essence which was constantly with you as the silent observer behind all experience. That which constitutes the unvarying fundament of your experience – the pure consciousness behind all experience – was constantly with you, but you were not there. Just as Meister Eckhart says, "God is within, but you are without."

In this dimension of consciousness, with crystal-clear awareness, you will realise that all you thought you had achieved on your whole spiritual path up to this point has been no more than a mass of empty shells. You have been playing with empty shells but you have not experienced the essence itself, you have not come any closer to the heart of the matter.

Do whatever you like: study philosophies, tackle Zen

texts, koans, and mondos as much as you please. But in your heart you still remain as lifeless as a corpse. You cannot find your true self through books and scholarliness because it lies beyond all words, beyond thought. You can study and memorise all the sacred scriptures and know all of the corresponding commentaries. The moment you suddenly awaken to the radiating truth of the Mind you will experience that all of this was nothing more than chaff, of no further value.

All this is just empty appearance and does not have the least to do with reality as it really is. Absolutely nothing! If you truly wish to put an end to your imprisonment in the circle of birth and death, you must cast away everything that you have ever held for important. Then you are free, even in the midst of birth and death. Nothing and no one can constrain you any longer and you come and go through birth and death like through an open door.

So why hesitate any longer? Why this constant coming and going, so that each time you appear here I am forced to ask again and again, "Who dragged this corpse here again for you today?" – this entire dead heap of interwoven memories, behavioural patterns, and thought models. That is why I sometimes greet you with the words, "I am so pleased that each one of you has turned up in such numbers today." We find a similar situation with old Joshu while greeting his disciples:

> Joshu went up to the lectern, stood there for a while and asked, "Has everyone arrived?"
> A monk replied, "They are all here."
> Joshu then said, "Let us still wait for one, and then begin with the lecture."

The monk said to this, "I pray inform the Master that no one else is expected."
Joshu replied, "It is hard to find a true one."

Let everything go, whatever it may be, and the ever-present reality of your true being will shine forth a hundred-thousand times brighter than the sun and will illuminate the entire universe with its light.

8

A Thunderclap In A Clear Blue Sky

MU MU MU MU MU
MU MU MU MU MU
MU MU MU MU MU
MU MU MU MU MU
Zen Master Mumon (thirteenth century)

This poem by the Chinese Zen Master Mumon was written in a measure of five characters. It is a wonderful Zen poem of extraordinary expressiveness. Mumon writes the character MU twenty times in succession.

What should we make of this? Does it have a deeper meaning or does he just want to make fools out of us? He could have written MU just once. That instead he wrote MU in a measure of five characters is everything but a Zenistic joke. The translation of MU is "nothingness" and Mumon's aim was to burn this nothingness into our hearts with the blazing seal of the buddha-mind. MU! MU! MU! MU! MU! Absolutely nothing – be absolutely dead! Die and be absolutely dead! Then do whatever you want; all is good!

The koan MU dates from the Chinese Zen Master Joshu. It is the most commonly used koan in Zen practise as it embodies a very strong force for transforming the mind. Let us now look at this wonderful koan MU from the old Master Joshu:

> A Zen monk asks Zen Master Joshu:
> "Does a dog have buddha-nature?"
> Joshu replies, "MU!"

Master Joshu's reply is simply "MU", "nothingness", which does not imply that a dog does not have buddha-nature. Joshu knew just as well as the monk that all beings without exception have buddha-nature, and thus we must not misinterpret Joshu's MU as a negation.

His only intention was to prevent the monk from wanting to understand Zen through rational thinking. Instead, he should be striving towards a higher perception of reality, "beyond affirmation and negation", in which all contradictions melt away of their own accord.

Joshu's MU is neither yes nor no. It is an alogical answer which surpasses the opposites, yes and no, and directly points to the buddha-nature; the absolute truth beyond all discrimination.

Here, Joshu's own experience of buddha-nature is creatively expressed in his MU. It points intensely to the incomparable Enlightenment experience which you can only reach when you have left all your discriminating thought behind you. Only when you are prepared to plunge into the abyss of the "Great Doubt" can the fullness of the divine void reveal itself to you.

If you are not ready for this, and believe you can solve the koan MU with your intellect, you will only end up in going round in circles, not advancing an inch. Those people who cling to words and sayings, interpreting MU with their intellect, and thus trying to understand it can be compared to a fool who tries to strike the moon with a stick.

The ancient masters said, "Attempting to solve MU in a rational way is like trying to pierce an iron wall with your fist." But what is the deeper meaning of Joshu's MU? The answer can only be, "Everything I could say of it would fall short of the mark", or in the words of

Huang-po, "All conceptual thought is erroneous belief." So why build a discussion on false concepts?

Whoever wishes to solve this koan, this MU problem, has no other choice than to bore into it with his whole being until he has become completely one with it. In his commentary on Joshu's MU Zen Master Mumon gives us the following advice:

> In Zen practise, the barrier raised by the ancient masters must be penetrated. Therefore, you must completely eradicate discriminating thought if you wish to attain Enlightenment. Now tell me: what is the barrier raised by the ancient masters? It is none other than this "MU". This is the Zen barrier, consequently known as the "gateless barrier" of Zen. Whoever overcomes this barrier will not only clearly see Joshu face-to-face, but can also walk hand in hand with all the masters of afore. Eyebrows touching, he sees with the same eye with which they see, and hears with the same ear with which they hear. Would it not be marvellous? Who doesn't wish to pass this marvellous barrier?
> Collect your strength in this "MU" and devote yourself to it day and night with your entire heart! Unceasingly proceeding in this way, your mind will suddenly become crystal clear like a burning candle which lights up the entire universe.

At the end of this in-depth commentary on Joshu's MU, Mumon adds a short poem to once again express MU. It is very direct and to the point:

Dog! Buddha-nature!
The truth is manifested in full.
A moment of yes and no:
Lost are your body and soul.

Here, Zen Master Mumon tells us most emphatically how to deal with the koan MU during Zen practise. His comment is from the Mumonkan, which he himself wrote, and which is one of the most important collections of koans.

For six years, Mumon practised fervently on the koan MU, and one day, as the great drum in the monastery was beat to announce midday, he suddenly experienced "Great Enlightenment". The following verses which he thereupon wrote express the intensity of this Enlightenment experience:

A thunderclap in a clear blue sky! All earthly beings have opened their eyes. Everything beneath the sun has bowed at once and Mount Sumeru jumps up and dances.

"*A thunderclap in a clear blue sky!*" The clear blue sky is the clear and empty condition of the Mind. When your mind is empty and clear, without thoughts and concepts, your true face before your birth will reveal itself. In the Avatamsaka Sutra it is written:

> If you wish to enter the realm of the enlightened ones you should make your mind as clear as empty space. Free yourself from all personal conceptions and all adhesion so that your mind is perfectly free, whatever it turns to.

When you have silenced your autonomous-turned, uncontrolled compulsive thinking, you will no longer produce the slightest trace of attachment and karma. Then you will already achieve complete freedom in this life. You really only need give up conceptual thought and you will have achieved everything.

When I speak of giving up conceptual thought, some of you may start to believe you must suppress all thinking and not allow a single thought to arise. But this is a huge mistake and utterly absurd.

Our sole matter of concern here is liberation from "compulsive thinking". When thinking has its practical value, you must of course make use of it. Yet when it becomes autonomous and compulsive, it must be stopped. It is a terrible malady, not being able to stop your thoughts, but since almost everyone suffers from this, you are unable to understand it and believe it to be a normal state of affairs.

Ruled by your autonomous-turned, uncontrolled compulsive thinking, you live in a state of separateness within a world of problems and conflicts. It is just like the dog in the hall of mirrors. It only sees its own projections, to which it reacts, filled with aggression and fear.

You are so identified with your intellect that you do not even realise that it has made a slave out of you. Your identification with the intellect causes you to derive your self-esteem from your intellect, and thus you fear that you will cease to exist if you stop thinking. Zen aims at breaking through this self-made vicious circle by achieving spiritual clarity.

Zen has nothing to do with discriminating thought. It has nothing to do with intellectual speculation. Rather, it is "pure experience", and thus a matter of inner perception. Zen is not one religion among many, but the foundation of all religions. Zen opens our eyes to the great mystery of our universal Essence.

It provides a path to the endless inner space which manifests itself to us in its endlessness beyond space, and its perpetuity beyond time. If the term "radically empirical" applies to anything at all, then it applies with certainty to Zen. Zen is pure experience in every respect. Take, for example, the following occurrence:

> One day as the Chinese Zen Master Ting was crossing a bridge, he encountered three highly learned Buddhist scholars.
> One of them wished to test Master Ting's understanding of Zen and asked him: "The river is deep and its depths must be plumbed. What does this mean?"
> The questioner had hardly finished speaking when Master Ting grabbed him with both hands and was about to throw him from the bridge. The other two scholars clutched his arms and begged him to let their friend go. Ting released the scholar and said: "If you had not held me back I would have let him plumb the depths of the river himself."

The highest truth is beyond all words and concepts, beyond all notions, all deliberation, all acceptance and rejection, all speculation, beyond all hopes and fears. It is beyond everything.

As long as you seek truth by using your intellect you cannot transcend it. In order to transcend it you must liberate yourself from your intellect with its entire accumulation of intellectual rubbish. Therefore, there is but one sole way for you to experience the truth, and that is: Free yourself of everything, whatever it may be, and the boundless expanse of the One Mind will manifest itself to you as the thunderclap in a clear blue sky! It is the "thunder of silence" which shakes the entire universe. The veil of maya, which has obscured your view of the awareness of your true being for incarnations until now, tears apart from top to bottom revealing the Holy of Holies, which was concealed behind it.

The Holy of Holies is the one brilliant Self-Mind. It is this one reality, beyond which nothing exists. At one fell swoop, your eye of Enlightenment opens, and for the first time, you see reality just as it is.

Mount Sumeru jumps up and dances.

"What?" A Mount jumps up and dances? What does this mean? In Buddhism, Mount Sumeru is the centre of the universe. And let me tell you that this centre is at the same time the core of your being, and thus the all-encompassing whole in which everything is contained.

Mount Sumeru is everything – the entirety. It is your true self and the boundless truth of divine being. Ageing, despair, illness, pain, and death; coming and going, diversity and unity – the entire dream of existence and non-existence dissolves and "Mount Sumeru jumps up and dances".

I am Mount Sumeru! You too are Mount Sumeru! There is no other Mount Sumeru. We are Mount Sumeru, for nothing exists besides the true self. The moment you awaken from the dream of "I" and world and space and time, there is nothing other than your original face before your birth.

All earthly beings have opened their eyes.
Everything beneath the sun has bowed at once.

Everything is an all-embracing entirety, containing everything within it. I am you and you are me, in our self we embrace the universe. My liberation means liberation for all beings.

In boundless Enlightenment, the whole world will appear before you as a wonderful abundance of glowing fairy-tale flowers. However, most Buddhists see things quite differently. They interpret the Bodhisattva vow which is recited daily in the Buddhist monasteries, "I vow to defer my liberation until all sentient being have found liberation" in completely the opposite way. In their limited dualistic view they cling to the external formulation and believe this to be true Bodhisattva consciousness. This is an entirely incorrect and extremely narrow conception. If one really had to wait the milliards of incarnations for all microorganisms, the tiniest living beings, to evolve into human beings and finally achieve liberation, then Enlightenment would be no more than a pipe dream. In this way, you remain forever caught in the wheel of birth and death, and never achieve liberation.

But "everything is the One Mind, besides which nothing else exists". Everything is One, and this One is everything, which, as written in the Lankavatara sutra, means that "Buddha loves all sentient beings because there are no sentient beings".

In truth, there is neither birth nor death. There is no coming or going, no imprisonment in samsara, and no liberation. Neither is there anything to acquire or achieve. In the words of Zen Master Huang-po:

> There is naught but a mysterious silent comprehension. – To suddenly become aware of the fact that your own mind is buddha, that there is nothing to achieve, and not a single activity to fulfil is the highest truth. Whoever grasps this is a buddha.

Let us now return to Zen Master Mumon's Enlightenment gata:

All earthly beings have opened their eyes.
Everything beneath the sun has bowed at once.

"All earthly beings have opened their eyes" – when your spiritual eye is open. That is why Meister Eckhart says, "The eye with which I see God and the eye with which God sees me is one eye, one seeing, one knowing, and one loving."

There is no longer any multiplicity, no other eye, no other seeing. There is just "one sole" seeing. "All earthly beings have opened their eyes" – all of them are liberated since everything is the One Mind, besides which nothing exists. The seer, the seeing, and that which is seen are one. I am you, and you are I. Whoever sees me, sees us. In our self we embrace the universe.

"Everything beneath the sun has bowed at once." Everything is One, and this One is everything. There is no multiplicity and thus no coming and going, no past,

no present, and no future. Nothing – MU! There is only an infinite, all-encompassing, boundless joy of being, an above-being divine nonbeing, beyond the capacity of conceptual denomination. This is your original face before your birth. "Everything I could say of it would fall short of the mark." And now, ... (Zensho raises his staff and is silent.) ... Do you hear it?

(short silence)

That is the true word. That is the thunder of silence! If you could hear it, this word in the ground of your being, in the absolute centre of here and now, then I would not need say any more and could be silent. To this, a Zen story:

In an old Chinese monastery of the Tang dynasty, the monks were in despair. It had been many weeks since the Master's last dharma lecture. The Master had retired to his dwelling and cloaked himself in silence. The monks began to chatter and asked themselves for what reason the Master had ceased his instruction. Finally the elder monks gathered and went to seek audience with the old Master.

One of them began to speak and said: "Venerable Master, all the monks in the monastery are very disquieted."

"Why? What is the problem?" asked the Master.

"You have stopped giving lectures. They would all like to have spiritual instruction again, a proper dharma lecture." "Well, if that's all it is, then sound the great bell! Everyone is to gather in the dharma hall." The great bell was rung. There was shouting and running, and everyone stormed excitedly into the dharma hall. They eagerly awaited the moment when the Master would enter the dharma hall. Finally the time came. The Master entered the hall, stepped up to the dharma pulpit and sat down on his high seat. After a moment's silence he began:

"Dear monks, dear assembly. There are highly learned philosophers who write thick volumes on Buddhism and Zen. Then there are commentators who compose long commentaries on these texts. And then there are the so-called teachers who comment on these commentaries. But I am a Zen master, and I ask you to bear this in mind!" With these words the Master rose and left the hall.

What a fantastic dharma lecture! Grandiose! Nothing can top it. A similar experience was had by the monks of Zen Master Huang-po:

On one occasion news travelled throughout the land that the great Master of Zen planned to deliver a great public dharma sermon and that all monks from neighbouring monasteries were invited to attend. They came from everywhere, near and far, by boat and raft, by donkey, horse, and on foot.

Many, of course, rode on cows – an important observation! An essential ascertainment. "They rode on cows!!!" Perhaps one day you will understand why I value cows so highly. Those who understand the relationship between the cow and Zen... But let us stick to the point. Whenever I speak of "cowology" I am in danger of straying from the subject.

So the news spread throughout the land and people came from everywhere. The dharma hall and courtyard were hardly big enough to accommodate the crowd of listeners that had gathered.

The big moment came. The bell was sounded and Zen Master Huang-po entered the Dharma hall and sat down on his high seat. After a moment's silence he began:

> Having many sorts of knowledge cannot compare with giving up seeking for anything. This is the best of all things! Mind is not of several kinds and there is no doctrine which can be put into words. As there is no more to be said, the assembly is dismissed!

Having spoken these impressive words, Huang-po stepped down from the high seat and left the dharma hall.

So, my dear friends, anything I could say of it would fall short of the mark. And since there is no more to say, today's assembly is also dismissed.

9

See Things As They Are

Today I have nothing special at all to tell you – not a word. For if I say even one single word, you are in danger of clinging to it.

You look at the word, define it, and relate it to your previous experiences. By doing so, you filter it through the screen of your old conditionings, behavioural patterns, and modes of thought; in other words, through all the woven-together memories of a dead past with which you identify yourselves. What comes out in the end has no longer any relation to the issue itself of which I spoke. And so it is better for me to remain silent.

(short silence)

But regardless of the danger I shall say a word. I shall say the word MU! In Zen MU means "nothing". Yet already you are clinging to this nothing. Each word causes your thoughts to arise, and when thoughts arise, all things arise.

One word, one thought and another thought, and already all problems have appeared, thus bringing a multitude of emotions with them. Yet when emotions arise, spiritual clarity is lost, and thus you create your own dualistic, multitudinous world of discrimination. And thus you end up living within a world of your self-made projections. You live in a world of joy or a world of suffering, in a world of conflict or a world of peace, depending on what you yourself create. Your mental state at any one moment corresponds exactly to the thoughts and emotions you momentarily bring forth. The German mystic Jacob Böhme (seventeenth century) describes this situation with the following words:

> Nothing is closer to you than paradise and hell – whichever you more tend to and try to reach is the one you are closest to. You have both of them within you.

Whatever we desire, we will become. This is the irrefutable karmic law of cause and effect. Now imagine: you are feeling good, are contented, and are lacking not the slightest thing.

Suddenly, for no reason, a memory surfaces from which you are unable to free yourself. Thought associations start to arise that lead to a series of emotional impulses, and before you know it, you are depressed, melancholic, or full of aggression. You are in your self-created hell. Yet externally, nothing has changed – it all takes place solely within you. You yourself project the world you experience.

Your discriminating, conceptual thinking has caused your self-made demons to appear, along with the whole satanic realm of greed, hatred, and blindness. However, these demons are not substantial beings. Instead, they are conditioned, and thus negative thought-associations which have become autonomous. They are brought forth by the "ego-delusion" and do not have an existence of their own, independent of the mind. If you can truly recognise this, you can transform your inner demons into the pure, crystal-clear awareness of the Mind.

It is this devil of ego-delusion which prevents you

from finding liberation. Yet not only is it the blatantly negative things which can become devils, or negative forces, when it is a question of freedom of the spirit, but also fond, benevolent friends and long-time companions too.

As long as you are yet to sever your ego-attachment, the inner demons will continue to be up to no good. Believe me; there is no greater devil than this clinging to the delusion of an "I".

"The true buddha-being is mysterious peaceful joy and that is all", says Huang-po. And this is your true nature. In the Viveka Chudamani, the fundamental Vedanta text, it is written: "You are Brahman, pure consciousness, the observer behind every experience, your true essence is joy."

In the Upanishads, the holy Indian scriptures, we read, "Brahman, pure divine Reality is Sat-Chit-Ananda" – absolute being, absolute consciousness, and absolute bliss. This is your true being. All the rest, that is to say, all the deluded thoughts you project out of desire and fear, is overlay. The following example demonstrates this:

In the evening you are walking along a path in the woods. Suddenly you see a snake lying across your way, and you run away horror-stricken. The next morning you go the same way and see – oh, it's only a rope!

Your fear projects a snake onto the rope lying on the ground. In the same way samskaras, your karmic formational forces, continuously project the delusion of an external phantom world with its myriad appearances and events. Yet all that is merely your own projection, for in truth, nothing exists besides the reality of the One Mind. This reality is ever present and is thus absolute "now". (Zensho strikes the ground with his stick!!!)

As you just heard, this "now" is also right "here". The thump when I strike the ground with this stick is not over there or yonder. The moment it sounds you cannot be there or elsewhere. That's it! That is the thunderclap of direct awareness, here-now! It is the sword of the Bodhisattva Manjushri which, with one stroke, cuts to pieces the chaos of your delusions.

Everything that causes all your daily problems has nothing at all to do with an adverse external world or its imperfect nature. Stop trying to find the cause of your suffering in external circumstances! The truth is that the cause of your suffering lies with you.

Whatever happens to you, whatever you encounter is a result of your own doing, and nothing more than your own projections. And there is not the slightest difference whatsoever between the three-dimensional world you experience during the day and the world you experience at night when you dream. Everything you experience in this "world dream" – this whole backdrop, the landscape, the living beings, all the problems, the joy and suffering, the coming and going, birth and death, everything, regardless of what it is – is your own projection.

That is why in the Mahayana-Samparigraha, a compendium of Buddhist Mahayana teachings from the fourth century, we read:

> The principle of the "mind-only-teaching" can be illustrated by comparing it with a dream and the dreamer. So long as you have not yet achieved Enlightenment and awoken to true wisdom, you have exactly the situation where you do not recognise your dreaming because you are still dreaming. As long as you have yet to awaken from

the dream of samsara (the circle of birth and death) you cannot truly understand the profound truth of the "mind-only-teaching".

Here-now! This is absolute reality, your true face before your birth. It is your true being, the reality of the One Mind. This One Mind, however, is the "Non-Mind". Non-Mind stands for the "true empty Mind". The true empty Mind lies beyond thought and is none other than shunyata, emptiness. In the Mahaprajnaparamita Hridaya Sutra, the Heart Sutra of Transcendent Wisdom, which is recited daily in Zen monasteries, it is written: "Form is emptiness and emptiness is form."

Form refers to everything you perceive. Everything – whether round or square, big or small, coloured, black or white – all that can form the content of your experience is empty.

Empty means lacking its own substance, having no being of its own. Consequently, the same applies to the six senses: sight, hearing, smell, touch, taste, and thinking. They are all "empty". And given that they are all empty, the product of the interplay of this sense-experience is no more than an illusion, having no reality whatsoever. If a causing factor lacks reality, then that which the factor causes, the end effect, lacks reality as well.

Hence, the problem of your imprisonment in a three-dimensional world can never be resolved by untying any one of the tiny individual knots of the Gordian knot of your spiritual confusion that you have tied so carefully over the course of untold incarnations. There is only one solution: Take the sword of Manjushri, the bodhisattva of non-discriminating wisdom and cut the Gordian knot to pieces with one stroke.

One lightening stroke with the sharp sword of non-discriminating clarity and you are free. One stroke, and your hundred thousand problems and troubles, all your delusions caused by dualistic discriminating thought fall apart. The Chinese Zen Master Hsueh-tou says this too:

> Where the sword of wisdom flies, sun and moon lose their shine and heaven and earth lose their colour. Through this experience the devils' bellies burst and the eye of transcendental wisdom opens to you.

There is no longer anyone who suffers, and no one who causes suffering. For if no one causes suffering, there can no longer be anyone who suffers. If you do not project anyone who attacks you, who assaults and threatens you, then there is no enemy for you to fight.

We are all familiar with Don Quixote, this somewhat dusty old knight who felt called upon to rid the world of evil. He sets off, and wherever he goes he sees enemies.

Take the windmills for instance. Believing them to be evil giants, he charges at them with his lance and fights until he winds up on the ground half-dead, his clothing torn to shreds.

You constantly battle your own projections. Just as you either fight or flee self-projected images when you dream, you do the same in samsara, the cycle of birth and death. The entire external world you experience has no independent reality of its own since it is merely your own projection. Samsara is a cyclical motion; it is the cycle of birth, ageing, despair, illness, pain, and death.

That is why Buddhism speaks of the bhava-chakra, the wheel of life.

In Buddhist iconography we often find the wheel of life of pratitya-samutpada, the circle of conditioned arising. At the hub of the wheel are the three kleshas: greed, hatred, and ignorance. As the three basic evils, they are the driving force behind the entire hocus-pocus conjured up by the human consciousness. The kleshas are depicted as a rooster, a snake, and a pig. The rooster stands for greed, the snake for hatred, and the pig that roots around in the mud, for ignorance.

Through ignorance – not recognising the deceptive nature of all phenomena – you project all sorts of notions. You then react to these projected notions with acceptance or rejection. As soon as something stands in the way of your self-projected object of desire, you react to this disturbance with aggression and rejection. This is how greed transforms into hatred, as a consequence of spiritual blindness. And thus this wheel of life of bhava-chakra continues to turn under the driving force of the three kleshas.

You cannot escape this situation by believing you can solve individual problems or by perhaps believing you can examine your past through psychotherapy, and then use the results to shed light on your present situation. Whatever it is you analyse is a dream occurrence, as is the process of analysis itself. There is no other way to liberation than to die out of this self-constructed prison of ego-armour.

"Die, ere you die, so that when you die, you will not be ruined", says Christian mystic Angelus Silesius. This is the only way. "To die out" means to awaken from the ego-engendered dream of samsara. Become absolutely nothing – "MU" – and you are awake! This is to surpass life and death and thereby to surmount all duality; accepting and rejecting, right or wrong.

"Your true being is mysterious peaceful joy and that is all", says Huang-po. Fantastic, wonderful! What is there to complain about? What is there to cry about? What is there to seek? Whom or what are you dream dancers chasing after? "Now", in the silence between the words of this lecture, if you do not project anything, you can perceive it, your true divine self which illuminates the whole universe with its light.

Forget yourself! Now, this instant – and Enlightenment is there. Meister Eckhart says: "Wherever thou art, leave thee there!" Leaving yourself is not something that you can do, in the sense of an action. Much rather, it is a matter of relaxing and forgetting yourself. It does not require any special effort. It simply means for you to fall into your own depths. The water drop falls into the ocean and dissolves into it.

Yet since you have become so accustomed to the dream you project, you have sadly come to the point where you no longer believe you can awaken to your true being. You come and listen to what I have to say to you and think, "It would be great if I could experience it." Yet in the process you completely forget that all I do is to hold up a large mirror before you that constantly reflects the reality of your Self-Being.

I never let myself become involved in your psychotic ego-games, even when time after time you attempt to lure me into your web of dreams. However, for your own good I sometimes appear to go with you into your dream and then, when we are dreaming together so pleasantly, I suddenly shout: "MUUUUU!!!"

This is then THE great opportunity for you to awaken out of your dream. For you are inside the dream and you are caught. But I am awake and completely free and only play along in your dream but I am not really in it. What is more, as Master I do not even exist! The master you perceive is the reflection of your true self. It is divine grace, which reveals itself to you through the veil of maya as "light in the darkness" in order to awaken you from your dream.

Had you not left the state of your original being, but instead had remained within yourselves, you would not be in the situation of coming to me today with the hope that I will reveal the truth to you. But I do not wish to keep you in suspense. I want to reveal to you today the highest truth. Believe me, today is a very special day! You will find out the truth... and the truth is: – Today is the 23rd, tomorrow is the 24th, and yesterday was the 22nd. And so I say to you: ...

(short silence)

Another great opportunity! My dear friends, I mean very well by you. Far better than you could mean with yourselves. For I do not let myself be deceived by all your identifications, by everything you believe yourselves to be.

I look directly into your hearts and see the true buddha, the perfectly enlightened one. Tat tvam asi – that you are. You are I, and I am you; in our self we embrace the universe. Whoever sees me, sees us. Everything is the One Mind, besides which nothing else exists.

Never forget that all your daily internal and external hardships are your own projections – without the slightest reality. If you do not understand this, your life will be a complete catastrophe. Just as riches attract more riches, bad luck attracts more and more bad luck. And since you are the ideal bearer, catastrophes will come to you from all over. That is why I give you the following crucial advice: always abide within yourselves, wherever you are.

When you truly abide within yourselves, in the awareness of Mind, what can endanger you, considering that there is no multiplicity? And who could threaten and harm you, considering that there are no living beings separate from one another? That is why the Lankavatara Sutra says: "Buddha loves all living beings because there are no living beings." There is truly only the one all-encompassing whole, this one multidimensional reality and nothing besides.

Take the sword of non-discriminating wisdom and shatter everything, whatever it be! Free yourselves of all your tender notions! Be it Christianity, Hinduism, Buddhism, or whatever.

Free yourselves of all grafted-on ideals and the burden of bygone illusions! – be they of nirvana, Enlightenment, the entire world – whatever they may be. Zen is completely free and does not tolerate a reliance on anything – not even Buddha. Zen Master Lin-chi says this too:

> Clear all obstacles from the path. If you encounter Buddha, then kill Buddha! Only thus will you attain release, only thus will you escape the chains and become free.

Shatter everything with the sword of wisdom, kill everything, and the dream of samsara, the circle of birth and death is over! You awaken, the light of the One Mind shines forth, and in a flash you experience that everything is just as it is – Tathata, the suchness of the One Mind.

Not since the universe came into existence has even a single speck of dust moved.

10

Be Here Now!

Students today lack self-confidence; they should not seek externally. As long as you continue to cling solely to the sayings of the ancient masters, you will never be able to distinguish between true and false.
ZEN MASTER LIN-CHI (NINTH CENTURY)

The ancient Chinese Zen Masters are magnificent, wonderful; they are brilliant. Their enlightened words reveal the profound truth of Zen and are of immeasurable value. Nevertheless, you should not forget that the truth you seek in the scriptures and statements of the ancient masters is nothing other than your own being.

You seek something that you yourself are – even though, tragically you have forgotten it, and no longer know who or what you are. That is why Zen Master Lin-chi begins with the words:

Students today lack self-confidence; they should not seek externally.

Zen Master Fen-yang (eleventh century) says:

Only very few people believe their own mind is buddha. Most do not take this seriously and thus are governed by their compulsions. They are surrounded by illusions, cravings, hatred, and other afflictions, all because they love the cave of ignorance.

Each of you has your own special perspective, a particular understanding of spiritual texts you study, of what you read or hear, yet it never amounts to more than a very limited point of view. All theories and reasoning which the intellect constructs are always limited and wrong. They are tied to discriminating conceptual thought and its narrow limits.

The intellect cannot be free from preconceived ideas because it too is made up solely of preconceived ideas. Using conceptual logic to comprehend the truth is, in the eyes of Zen, nothing more than ignorance. Relying on your discriminating conceptual thought means preventing the inner light from unfolding.

Whatever can be achieved through thought is inevitably naive and egocentric, and is only ever of superficial and temporal value. The same goes for all the various philosophies and religions. They are all just very "limited perspectives" of the inexpressible truth, but never the truth itself. On this subject there is an old Indian tale:

Five blind men meet an elephant driver seated on an elephant's back. They ask him, "We are blind and thus have never seen an elephant. May we touch your elephant to find out what it looks like?" "As you wish", says the elephant driver.

The first man feels the trunk and exclaims, "Well I never! The elephant looks like a thick hose!"

The second touches the elephant's ear and declares, "You are wrong, the elephant looks like a big fan!"

The third grasps hold of the tail and says: "No, the elephant looks like a thin rope!"

The fourth grasps the leg and proclaims: "Totally wrong, the elephant looks like a tree stump!"

Finally, the fifth touches the elephant's belly and says, "You are all wrong. The elephant looks like a huge barrel!"

Upon hearing this, the elephant driver says: "None of you is right. Each of you has grasped only a part of the whole but none of you has discerned what the elephant really looks like."

Similarly, all statements of the various religions and philosophies should be understood in this light. Only once you dive directly into the ocean of wisdom yourselves, into the boundless ocean of the One Mind, will you come to know the truth. Do you want to know what water is? Drink it – or jump into the water! This is the way of Zen.

Zen does not offer any philosophical explanations. Zen says: "If you want to know how tea tastes – drink it! Do you want to know how an apple tastes? Then take a bite of the apple! Then you know: that's how it is." That is pure Zen. Zen is always immediate and direct. With the greatest emphasis, it constantly points to your own heart, without becoming caught in the tangle of conventions and concepts. It is free, and without this freedom it loses its spontaneity and freshness, ending up as just a dead, empty shell, devoid of all life.

Zen always points to the pure naked truth. It wastes no time with external aesthetic chitchat or with mind-bending speculation. It cannot be expressed in words. It has nothing to do with pious pretensions and the accumulation of intellectual refuse. Zen means: "to immerse oneself" – to immerse oneself in the One. This One is the reality of which Huang-po says:

All buddhas and all sentient beings are nothing but the One Mind, beside which nothing else exists.

This small apposition, "... beside which nothing exists", is most essential, since the One Mind is the all-pervading entirety of all presumed multiplicity. All the waves on the surface of the ocean are the ocean itself. The movement of the waves, the various forms of the waves, the many white crests and the bubbles on top – this entire endless diversity of coming and going is the one ocean.

Every perception of multiplicity is due to the mistaken perception of your dualistic consciousness, which leads to the delusion of a pseudo-individuality. This pseudo-individual, the ego, is no real being and has no true being of itself.

The ego has no existence of its own and is merely a process. It is a process in the form of identification with the memories of a dead past, with old patterns of behaviour, and with countless notions and concepts. But that is not what you are. It has not the slightest to do with what you really are at the ground of your being.

Yet in your spiritual blindness you nonetheless believe this to be you, and are convinced that all others are this way too. What is more, you believe the external world to be what your senses perceive.

In truth, you only appear to perceive external things through your sense organs because space is no more than a projection of your consciousness. You may believe you are moving in a three-dimensional world in space and time, but in fact it is only the mind that moves.

The mind is the fundament of everything, and everything takes place only in the mind. Since accordingly, the prerequisite for external perception is lacking, every external perception is thus an internal, purely mental process. In the Lankavatara Sutra, one of the most important scriptures of Mahayana Buddhism, it is written:

> What appears to be external does not exist in reality; it is indeed just Mind, seen in multiplicity. Body, possessions, and the world – all these are nothing but Mind.

Everything we perceive in the world, including the apparent solidity of material, is accordingly nothing more than an illusory notion of the mind.

Everything is but Mind – there is neither within nor without. What you actually perceive is the space-timeless dimension of the Mind, but you fail to recognise this because it is overshadowed by the karmic driving forces.

The karmic driving forces are the entire process of identification, attachment and diversification that I have just described. Taking this for the world, you say: "This is the world in which we live. In this world of suffering of birth, ageing, despair, illness, pain, and death, we are trapped. How can we possibly escape?"

In fact, you are not trapped at all. The idea of being trapped is just a thought. You have stirred up a mind game, a dream vision, a web of maya. You have entangled yourselves in it and are unable to free yourselves.

Yet, since everything is no more than a web of thoughts, freeing yourselves from it can only mean taking the sword of non-discriminating realisation and slicing through the Gordian knot of your spiritual confusion – and the problem is solved. To put it better: the problem is neither solved nor is it not solved – for there was no problem at all. It was only an illusion!

What do you lack then? The only thing you lack is trust in your true self. Since you are lacking this trust, you seek externally for this truth which is within you. That is why, in our starting quote, Lin-chi says:

> *Students today lack self-confidence; they should not seek externally. As long as you continue to cling solely to the sayings of the ancient masters, you will never be able to distinguish between true and false.*

What is meant here is this indisputable trust in your own immanent divine reality. It is the deep-rooted belief which matures into that absolute certainty that things are just as the enlightened masters and all awakened ones of all times and regions have proclaimed.

The master's words are fingers that point to the moon. The moon is reality, the finger is merely the signpost, but you study the finger and cling to it. You study the various systems of instruction, philosophies, and religions, and take them for the truth, yet they are all just worthless junk, intellectual refuse – nothing! The moon is the truth, not the finger. Never forget this. That is why Zen Master Yang-shan (ninth century) says:

> I explain you things which relate to Enlightenment but do not attempt to let your mind linger on them. Turn to the ocean of your own being and bring yourselves in accordance with its true nature.

The illumination of the Self-Mind beyond all speculation and perception, beyond the supposed external world – that is the reality you seek!

This is the true condition of the boundless, ultramundane One Mind. All else is illusion. And so: leave everything behind! "Let the dead bury their dead", and surrender yourselves fully to the divine being! This is the only way to liberation! Zen Master Lin-chi says:

> A righteous man discusses neither rulers nor rebels, neither right nor wrong, neither beauty nor wealth. He does not spend his days discussing empty words.

This means: the true man of Zen leaves things just as they are. The political factors of a world situation do not disturb him in the least; just as little as all the other factors which are of such indispensable importance for the average worldly-bound person.

The true man of Zen does not differentiate between right and wrong and is not interested in riches and possessions; all these are things that do not have the slightest meaning for him. They are all simply reflections of your fears and desires – reflections of attachment and rejection, resulting from your spiritual blindness.

The reflections of a manifold world with all its problems amount to no more than overlay, obscuring the reality of the Self-Mind. How do you wish to free yourselves of it? You cannot free yourselves by seeking here and there. (Zensho stomps his staff on the floor!!!)

This is it! Everything is here. Right "now" in this instant there resounds the thunderclap in a clear blue sky.

Whoever immerses himself entirely in here and now sees his true face before his birth – the birthless and deathless Self-Being.

In today's esoteric funfair, however, the expression "here and now" has become a worn out catchphrase. "Here and now" can be found in almost every book of the "esoteric wave". Be it in the writings of modern western success-gurus, or in the books and workshops of psychologists and therapists. Everyone talks about "here and now".

But when you really understand what Zen is all about, you will recognise that this whole esoteric "here and now talk" is utter nonsense and has nothing at all to do with the "here and now" of Zen. It is just as I always say, "Esoteric is only for dimwits."

Here is now! And that is eternity. You are always in eternity, even if you are not aware of it. Your thoughts produce the notion of time. Pure consciousness, however, "now-here", is beyond the process of changing. In the absolute presence of Here and Now, the Eternal reveals itself.

11

The Eternal Tao

The speakable Tao is not the eternal Tao.
The mentionable name is not the eternal name.
The nameless is the beginning of heaven and earth.
The named is the mother of the myriad beings.
And so:
Constant non-desire views the most secret.
Constant desiring views only the limited.
LAO-TSE (SIXTH CENTURY B.C.)

Lao-tse was one of the most significant Chinese masters and is revered as the founding father of Taoism.

His book, the Tao Te King, "the holy book of Tao", is regarded as the foundation work of Taoism. The text we are going to speak about today is taken from this book and appears right at the start of the first chapter. It begins with the following words:

The speakable Tao is not the eternal Tao.
The mentionable name is not the eternal name.

Everything of which can be spoken belongs to things which exist and do not exist, to the categories of being and non-being. For whatever names and circumlocutions you may ascribe to the inconceivable, and thus unspeakable origin of all being, in the end they are but your own limited conceptions and images of the Tao, but never the Tao itself.

Tao is intangible and indefinable since defining means setting limits. It is a concept for something which defies all conceptualisation. All attempts to force the Tao into conceptual forms are as if one would attempt to capture heaven in a net. "Not doubting words is a terrible malady", says Zen.

All thought is an erroneous belief, and the result of it is nothing but empty concepts. However, behind thought there is the Eternal, which lights up the entire universe with its radiating light. It is that which always is, has been, and will be. But the "speakable" Tao, that is to say, the conceptual fixation of the unspeakable reality, is never more than a shadow, an arbitrary conceptual designation. That is why the Christian mystic Meister Eckhart says:

> Everything you can say about God is by no means God at all. No one can reach what God in his self is who has not been translated into a light which is God himself.

Whether I say God, Buddha, or the Absolute, everything I say, whatever it is, falls short of the mark. It has not the slightest to do with what lies beyond everything that sense and reason can comprehend. All your efforts to force the One Mind, besides which nothing else exists, into conceptual forms are completely futile, achieving nothing.

The One Mind is unfathomable and indefinable. Every definition reduces the inexpressible to a dualistic, limited perspective. Defining means reducing something to specific predefined limits. Therefore it can only be narrow and limited, thus excluding all else.

All efforts of discriminating thought to understand something must, by its inherent nature, be reductive and limiting. In view of this lamentable nature of the intellect, we should not be surprised that the pure truth of Zen eludes all intellectual examination. This nature of Zen, which the intellect cannot conceive, is clearly illustrated in the following example:

> A monk asked Zen Master Yun-men: "What is the essence of a patched-robe monk's existence?"
> The master replied, "It's your turn."
> The monk did not know what to do with the answer, so he begged, "Master, please tell me."
> Yun-men then said, "Playing zither for a cow."

The nameless is the beginning of heaven and earth.

The beginning of heaven and earth, as Lao-tse puts it, is not something we should interpret here as being the beginning of some endless timeline. It is not the beginning of some continuous sequence of events and happenings, however long they may be and when they began, which you then call evolution or the emergence of the universe.

There is neither space nor time, coming nor going, nor is there a sequence of consecutive events. For everything is a "simultaneity", without before and without after, without beginning and end.

There is no beginning. Space and time are no more than the erroneous perception of your discriminating, conceptual consciousness. The nameless is the boundless, and thus the beginningless. It is the unborn and deathless One Mind, besides which nothing else exists. In the words of old Lao-tse:

> There is a being, intangible, sublime.
> It precedes heaven and earth,
> so silent, so formless.
> Alone in itself, unchanging,
> all-pervading, everlasting.
> It can be called the mother of the universe.

This primordial mind is endless and without bounds. In its perfect limitlessness it fills the entire universe with piercing radiance.

The named is the mother of the myriad beings.

The process of increasing consciousness which the mind undergoes in terms of its own existence leads to the perception of a spatially dispersed world of individuation.

The moment conceptual fixation arises, be it only the faintest hint of an initial impulse, limitation is there. Your perception is limited in just the same way when you look through a drinking straw. This is the dualistic perspective through which the reality of the all-encompassing whole – the boundless expanse of the One Mind – contracts to a microcosmic partial aspect of the cosmic Mind. It is a contraction of consciousness into the pseudo-existence of an ego which experiences itself as separate from all else.

But since everything is the One Mind, beside which nothing else exists, the named is identical in essence to the nameless, yet different in appearance. The named is conceptual fixation and thus, all things come into being, meaning: the illusion of multiplicity arises. In the words of Zen Master Huang-po:

When thoughts arise, all things arise and when thoughts disappear, all things disappear.

That is why Lao-tse says:

Constant desiring views only the limited.

Desiring is wanting to possess, wanting to grasp and to cling, caused by ignorance. For where there is ignorance, there is also the tendency towards acceptance and rejection.

That is why Buddhist teaching designates desire, hatred, and ignorance as the three basic evils from which samsara, the circle of birth, ageing, despair, illness, pain, and death emerges. This basic condition is the root of all evil.

"Constant desiring views only the limited", because desiring sets limits. Your life resembles that of a fly which has become trapped in a narrow bottle. Sweet fragrance has enticed it into the bottle and feverishly, it flies around in search of a way out. In its desperate attempt to come out it hits the glass again and again, and sees that freedom is close at hand.

Most people are caught in this situation. Due to their constant desiring they find themselves in a state which prevents them from leading a free life. Constant desiring is caused by spiritual blindness; ignorance, which generates more and more ignorance. Thus the veil of maya, the illusion of a manifold external phenomenal world in space and time, becomes increasingly dense.

And so you have become entangled in this net of desire, hatred, and ignorance. The more you try to break free, the more each attempt at liberation will lead you to become increasingly bound. In so doing, you entangle yourselves more and more in this miserable, pitiable state of contracted consciousness which you yourselves have brought about. This is the limitedness which Lao-tse means when he says, "Constant desiring views only the limited."

What I am about to tell you now can easily be misunderstood – just like so many things I say: This desiring, specifically the inner driving force of desiring, is at the same time – and this is a very important point – the unconscious impulse in every person towards divine reality. Each of us seeks but knows neither that he seeks nor what he seeks. That is why Saint Augustine (fifth century) says:

Restless is our heart until it rests in God.

You seek and rush around in spiritual restlessness, just like a monkey turned wild, jumping from one branch to the next. You seek and seek, without knowing what you are seeking. You fail to realise that what you seek is actually the innermost driving force of your seeking itself. It is your true self, which is superimposed by the delusion of an ego with the world it experiences. Consequently, all external seeking is a misinterpretation of what you are really seeking, brought about by your ignorance.

You seek externally for something you can only find within. Since all you achieve through external seeking cannot give you any ultimate fulfilment, you remain inwardly hollow and dissatisfied. Finding no true fulfilment, you set your goals ever higher. All your endeavours to build up a state of lasting contentment on the fleeting joys of this dream-world must inevitably end in disappointment. For this reason, Bodhidharma (sixth century), the first patriarch of Zen Buddhism says of this:

> Wherever you have desiring, you will find suffering. When desiring ceases, you will be free from suffering. Non-desiring is the path to truth.

By not recognising reality, you are plagued by all sorts of cravings for this and that, all for the sake of snatching a short moment of fleeting happiness. This leads you to become increasingly entangled in all sorts of addictions. Alcohol, sex, and pleasant things are neither good nor bad, but the fatality of it is that you very quickly become addicted to them.

It is just the same with porcupines which crawl into rat holes. They can enter very easily, but it is impossible for them to come out again, however much they try. They are stuck and cannot escape.

Clinging to transitory things just for the sake of a moment's fleeting illusion of happiness only brings new karma. All situations and events in your life are the result of foregone thoughts and acts.

Every action in the present dictates your destiny to come. Thus, your whole life is an unfolding of karma. It is a constant, repeating series of cause and effect.

Karma, however, means obstacles, and therefore suffering. So do not cling to impermanence. Nothing impermanent can bestow true, lasting happiness on you. For everything is transitory, and transitoriness is suffering. Buddha says:

> This world will come to pass and all that seems important is fleeting. You must each awaken from your dream. There is no time to lose and thus:
> Be steadfast in your efforts! All existence is impermanent like autumn clouds. Birth and death are like scenes from a play on the stage of life. Life passes like a flash of lightening in the sky, it passes like a torrent rushing down the mountainside.

The Japanese Zen poet Ryokan Daigu (nineteenth century) describes the impermanence of all existence with the following poetic words:

> Someday I shall be a decaying skull,
> rotting on the grass somewhere.
> Perhaps a dog will come by,
> to pee on it or take a sniff,
> or one or two passing birds
> will pause briefly on it,
> to quickly chirp a little melody.
> Rulers and simple folk
> end up the same –
> passing like a dream after the night.

This world is fleeting. But you do not suffer because everything in the world is fleeting. You suffer because you cling to impermanence.

The reason for your suffering is not because the world is not right but because you are not right. By not recognising the deceptive nature of all appearances you move incessantly from one birth to the next, obsessed by the delusion of countless fantasies formed by the empty phantasmagoria of thought. And so you wander aimlessly, searching on the outside without knowing what you seek, for it is only to be found at your innermost self.

At the innermost place of the heart the clear light of the Mind shines. Yet continual desiring only looks to the external and creates limitation. Through desire, you bind yourselves within your self-created limitation. Thus you give rise to the illusion of an independent, self-existing individuality, which is no other than limitation.

Let us now return to Lao-tse's preceding statement. I began by commenting on the second statement so that you better understand the first one.

Constant non-desire views the most secret.

"Constant non-desire" is a complete letting go of yourself and all things. However, it is not a letting go in the sense of something you do, rather, in the sense of letting things happen. This is the true meaning of the Taoist wu-wei, non-action.

Meister Eckhart says: "God acts and I become." Yet for God to act on you, you must first cease acting. As long as you yourself still act, and with the help of discriminating conceptual thought, wish to understand the mystery of being, God does not act. He says, "Great, fantastic, that's wonderful, how wise you are with all your knowledge and dealings. If you think you can do it yourself then be my guest, I shall not stand in your way."

Constant non-desire views the most secret.

When you are free from every desire and abide in inner non-action, leaving everything just as it is, you place no limitations. When you no longer limit, you do not fixate anything, and thus you have no fixed perception.

Having no fixed perception means: you no longer view the world through your stencil of a dualistic perspective of acceptance and rejection. You become free of your old accustomed patterns of behaviour and thought models. You become free of your bygone memories of a dead past and your fears for the future and everything is good just the way it is.

"Every day is a good day", says Zen. Thus you proceed through all the ups and downs of daily life without constantly becoming embroiled in all sorts of self-made problems.

Free of the burden of your old illusions, nothing can deceive you any longer, and you live your life in complete freedom.

12

Love Is The All-Embracing Whole

There are two forms of love: love in the form of having and love in the form of being.

Love in the form of having is a pseudo-love that manifests itself in a quick emotional stirring, in a fleeting impulse. I shall illustrate this with an example:

While walking in a meadow you suddenly come upon a beautiful flower. You pick it and take it home with you because you are in love with the flower. At home you put it in a vase – and three days later you throw it into the rubbish bin. This is love in the form of having.

Yet, in truth, this is not love at all but rather it is the desiring of the ego misinterpreted as love. You see an object, desire it and want to grasp this object – that is what is called "having".

This is not the case with love in the form of being – with pure love. Pure love is love in the form of all-encompassing entirety. It does not become caught up in the conditioned, emotional impulses of dualistic discrimination.

It is not a pseudo-love that wants to grasp and possess, but indeed quite the opposite. It is love which gives of itself and surrenders itself, just like the moth that sees an open flame and, forgetting itself, flies into the flame. Pure love constantly seeks to remove all opposites since it strives to perfect unity. "Love begins where thinking ceases", for it is beyond all opposites. Meister Eckhart speaks of this when he says:

> The eye with which I see God and the eye with which God sees me – this is one eye, one seeing, one knowing, and one loving.

Here, all duality is dissolved. Love is the all-encompassing whole that contains everything within itself.

Yet wherever you, in your egocentricity, step out from the whole, from the universal entirety, by segregating yourself and calling attention to yourself and feeling important, you step out from all-encompassing love.

Segregation always means a state of dividedness, and leads to separateness. This separateness arises from the duality of acceptance and rejection, and escalates to greed, hatred, and ever increasing spiritual blindness. This dualistic mentality of discriminating ignorance is also the reason for all the disagreement in the world. In total contrast to this are the Buddhist principles on the liberation from dualistic conceptions:

> Do not take the knowledge you currently possess to be the absolute unchanging truth. Avoid being narrow-mindedly trapped in your current viewpoint. Learn and practise non-attachment to conceptions, so that your perception is open to the viewpoints of others.

Discriminating ignorance always produces resistance which is inseparably tied to the intellect. Yet relinquishing this resistance leads to surrender. All forms of judging and all negativity dissolve and the reality of pure being, which the intellect has been covering, opens to you.

Pure love, which surrenders itself completely, manifests itself in self-forgetting love of the eternal. There is no ego-intellect and thus no wanting for oneself. For this reason Jesus prays in the garden of Gethsemane shortly before his Crucifixion: "Father, if thou wilt, let this cup pass from me; nevertheless not as I will, but as thou wilt!"

This surrender culminates in its radical self-renunciation on the cross. And thus, the attitude of mind of the crucified person is that of man's total devotion to the reality beyond being of the divine being.

At this point on the cross Jesus cries out the words that have confused many a Christian mind: "Eli, Eli, lema sabachtani?" that is to say, "My God, my God, why hast thou forsaken me?"

Most Christian theologians interpret this statement as follows: They see it as a show of Jesus' human helplessness as he hangs on the cross and, in his abandonment, doubts the existence of God.

They believe that, for a brief moment, Jesus loses his belief in the God in whom he has trusted, such that in great despair and fear of death he cries out: "My God, my God, why hast thou forsaken me?" However, this is a completely wrong interpretation.

The mystical meaning, the truth behind these words is totally different. It goes much deeper than the limited dualistic perspective of theological scholarliness can imagine here. For when Jesus cries out on the cross: "My God, my God, why hast thou forsaken me?" it is altogether different than if he had said: "Oh my, oh my, here I hang on the cross with hands and feet pierced right through. I trusted in a higher power that probably doesn't exist. It has all been for nothing; I have been taken in by a fraud." No, that is not what he says! Instead he appeals directly to this power in which he trusts by addressing it in saying, "My God, my God, why hast thou forsaken me?" Only one who is certain of the existence of divine reality would address it in this way. No one in his right mind would address such words to someone whom he believes does not even exist.

The words of the dying Jesus on the cross: "... why hast thou forsaken me?" are indeed a cry of abandonment, but they are not words that doubt the existence of divine reality. For the moment Jesus cries: "My God, my God, why hast thou forsaken me?" he likewise underlines his irrefutable faith in God, by whom he no longer feels supported, and thus he feels abandoned by him.

This is the moment of mystical death. In this process of releasing yourselves from space and time, you find yourselves in "the dark night of the senses and the mind".

You no longer have the one, the feeling of stability in the world – and you are yet to have the other, absolute reality; and this is a tremendous state of spiritual vacuum. You feel how space and time dissolve, such that you no longer find anything to hold on to. And so you jump back fearfully, afraid that you will be drawn into the bottomless abyss of the void and will not return to life. In the words of the Chinese Zen Master Huang-po:

> Those who hasten towards the void dare not enter, fearing to hurtle down through the void with nothing to cling to. So they gape at the deep abyss they cannot overlook and retreat horrified. They are afraid to empty their minds. They fear they may plunge into the void and do not know that their own mind is the void.

The words of Jesus: "... why hast thou forsaken me?" are a koan for the whole of humankind. They are a call to directly follow him "here and now". It is just like when the young man comes and asks Jesus what he must do to become his disciple and Jesus says, "Come and follow me!" To this the young man replies, "Alright, but I'm afraid it won't be right away for my father has died and I must bury him first. I have a lot to do right now: I must order the grave, organise the funeral service, then I have to …" And Jesus interrupts him and says, "Amen, I say to you, let the dead bury their own and follow me!"

Follow me "now"! (Zensho strikes his staff on the floor!!!) Now! Not some other time, not tomorrow or the day after, for only Now exists. Tomorrow and the day after are only a thought, an empty concept, just like the other thousands of empty concepts that you all have in your heads.

When you are not caught in the future or in the past, and you are not tied to things in the present you will recognise that everything is completely empty and without reality. Do not hold on to the past and do not brood over the future, otherwise you will only end up trapping yourselves in phantasms, and your mind will become confused.

When I speak of Now there is the danger that you will also turn this Now into an empty concept and say, "I still have to achieve this Now." As a consequence, you have shifted this Now into the future and have missed its absolute presence. You can only experience Now when you become aware and clearly recognise – Now is already here! Never say I still must achieve this Now, since Now is always here.

Now is always here, but "you" are not here. Now is always present, but you are not present. You do not need to go anywhere in order to experience Now. All you must do is to immerse yourself in the immediate presence of Now. Stop covering the absolute presence of your true being with the rubbish your deceptions produce! Let go of everything – forget yourself!

The moment you surrender yourselves to the Absolute and die into the great death, you enter the great darkness – the dark abyss of the divine void. Everything melts away, all your conditionings and all your exasperating mental concepts and ideals. The curtain in the temple, as the veil of maya – the illusion of space and time, of birth, ageing, despair, illness, pain, and death – tears apart.

Everything dissolves away and sets the Holy of Holies free. This Holy of Holies is your true face before your birth, the reality existing of itself, which you have always been and shall ever be. You yourselves are the temple. "Do you not know that you are the temple of the Holy Spirit?" says Saint Paul. Throw everything out of the temple, all these conditionings and dead concepts, all the programming and slogans that you have drummed into your heads and have had drummed into you by others over the course of your whole lifetime.

Throw it all out, whatever it is! Away with it! Just like Jesus does when he goes into the temple, turns over the tables, and chases out the moneychangers and dove sellers with the cry: "Be gone with you! You have turned my Father's house into a den of thieves. Away with you!" And then it is silent in the temple.

Not until there is silence within you will your true being beyond all words reveal itself. Yet as long as there is still something within you in the form of acceptance and rejection, right and wrong, this, that and whatever, you cannot hear the tone of silence. For it is pure being, just as it is. In the language of Zen: "It is the One without second." And because it is the One without second it does not tolerate anything besides itself. As long as there is still something in your consciousness – be it even the tiniest notion – you are still heavens away from the divine reality of your true being.

In complete self-surrender to the abyss of the divine darkness which appears as the fullness of the Great Life, pure love in its entirety reveals itself. That is why Saint John the Evangelist says:

> God is love, and he who abides in love abides in God and God in Him.

The reality beyond being is the all-embracing wholeness of being. It is the entirety which contains everything within itself. It is the one inseparable whole, which recognises and loves itself in all seeming multiplicity.

God – or in the language of Zen: the One Mind – is love. Whoever abides in this love – in this whole, in this non-duality, in this non-separation – abides in the reality of the One Mind, and the reality of the One Mind in him. But the moment you take anything away, believing that it does not belong to the total harmony of being, you step out of love. You lose love.

Yin and yang, life and death, beautiful and ugly, good and bad, everything is the all-embracing totality of being. The connection; that is to say, the reciprocal causation and mutual penetration of yin and yang, is the working of Tao. Tao flows like water. If you do not stand in opposition to anything, whatever it is, then you are in harmonic flow with the whole – in accord with Tao. And thus you dwell in all-encompassing divine love. This love is as strong as death. Meister Eckhart says:

> Not only is love as strong as death, it is indeed much stronger than death, for it even knows how to kill death.

Just as death tears you away from everything and destroys everything, so too does love. Whoever abides in all-embracing love will experience everything as this pure love, or in the words of Meister Eckhart: "Everything becomes supreme God." He now sees nothing but the Divine, he sees nothing but pure reality wherever he goes, wherever he stands, everywhere. When you abide in this love, you are beyond life and death, for everything is then One.

The whole universe, coming and going, life and death – everything, whatever it may be, is the fullness of pure being. And if you live in and out of this fullness of eternal being, you are free of all anxiety and fear. Death is then not the final word. It is no longer this dark menace which will tear you away from your pleasant life for you to fall into a dark empty void.

As the hand of divine love, it raises you up into the blazing light of the Mind – the reality of your birthless and deathless Self-Nature.

13

No Zen Without Enlightenment

Each religion and each philosophy is just a means of assistance, "a finger that points to the moon", as the Lankavatara Sutra puts it. Yet the finger must not be confused with the moon to which it points.

The highest truth is very simple, but people cling unnecessarily in their spiritual searching to all sorts of external teachings and practises.

You go to a lot of trouble with all the different ways and methods, trying to reach something that you can never achieve. Therefore, Zen Master Huang-po says of this:

> Only by preventing conceptual thought from arising will you achieve Enlightenment. Then you will also experience buddha, who has always been present in your own mind. All the eons of fervent seeking will prove to have been equally long spent in wasted effort.

You are seeking something that you can never find because you have never lost it.

It is just like the old Indian parable of the man wearing a headband with a valuable pearl on it and who suddenly thinks he has lost this pearl. He runs from one place to the next, searching in despair for his valuable pearl until finally, he looks in the mirror and realises: what he has been seeking has been there the whole time – he had never lost it. The truth is purely a matter of recognising, and not one of acquiring anything. In the

Hsin-hsin-ming, one of the principle Zen texts from the seventh century, it is written:

> The highest truth is not difficult and allows no preferences. When you no longer hate or desire, it reveals itself clearly and infinitely.
> Yet whoever remains separate from it, be it by even a hair's breadth, is so far apart as the heavens from the earth.
> And so: you need not seek the truth, just silence your thoughts – this is all that matters.

Open your eyes, leave everything just as it is, stop running about like startled chickens and see things for what they are!

When you leave everything just as it is, it means that you no longer place a stencil of conceptual fixation over things, the stencil of your old concepts. It means you no longer distort situations and things with any kind of recollections; that is to say, with memory contents of a dead past, and then believe that which you project to be the thing itself.

It is just the same as if you would see a rope at night in the moonlight lying alongside a path, and in a state of panic, you project the notion of a snake onto it. Terrified, you back off and run away. Yet the next day when the sun is shining you pass along the same way and you see: it was only a rope.

The sunlight of clear realisation shows you the truth, so that you see things just as they are. Nothing is projected onto it, and everything is clear, and everything is good just the way it is. "Every day is a good day", says Zen.

The pure nature of Being, which forms the base of everything, is gloriously radiating peaceful joy. It is open and clear, without limits and bounds. Everything is a revelation of divine reality. Everything is filled with the fullness of God.

Yet one thought of grasping and already you are caught up in desire. And one thought of rejecting and already you are filled with anger and rejection.

The true attitude of mind is one of inner equanimity. The more relaxed you become, the more your world will become peaceful in a very natural way. This happens because you achieve cheerful serenity when you inwardly let go and gradually come into unison with your true being, and thus with the all-embracing whole. Abiding in yourself, you move within a world of apparent multiplicity and are able to leave things just as they are.

It is a completely wrong attitude to conceptually fixate the world and categorise it in terms of good or not good. It is wrong to believe the external world must be altered in order for you to feel good, and living in the world is a hindrance on the spiritual path. You are making a huge mistake if you believe you must give up an active life in the everyday world in order to reach spiritual realisation. This is a very limited perspective.

A perspective is always a limited viewpoint. It is only a single point of view to the exclusion of all other points of view, and this means: you are viewing through the end of the drinking straw of contracted consciousness. The boundless expanse of the One Mind contracts to a microscopic partial aspect – the viewpoint of the ego.

The world, the situation in which you find yourselves in life, is neither good nor bad, neither right nor wrong. You yourselves, in your conditioned perspective project all sorts of notions onto what you see, that is to say, onto all that you encounter.

In this way, you project all your memories, the ancient contents of your dead recollections, onto the situation and react in an accustomed way with acceptance or rejection, blindly believing that things really are as they appear to you.

Let us take the following example: You see a young woman, beautiful and pure as a flower. Yet in your lust for her you project all sorts of sexual desires onto her, and see nothing more in her than a sex object that you desire. But that is not the world as it is. That is not suchness but rather, it is you in your I-delusion.

The ego projects and creates its own world. Yet this world of the ego is no more than an endless coming and going of wishes and fears, of thoughts and feelings, and thus the cycle of birth and death. This cycle of birth and death is no other than a psychical projection of consciousness.

You will only recognise reality as it is when you have firstly awakened from this habitual misinterpretation and the resulting misperception. Then you will be the Tathagata, the thus-come one, who sees things the way they are. Then you are buddha, the fully awakened one, who comes, goes, eats and drinks, just as he pleases.

Yet, achieving this requires the spiritual guidance of an enlightened master. However, when you begin your search for a true master in today's giant maze of spiritual paths, you will encounter thousands upon thousands of masters, both self-proclaimed, and nominated by others. It is these pseudo-gurus who show off with pleasant words and just parrot what they have read or heard from others. In the words of Zen Master Yun-men:

> There is a band of phrase mongers who slurp up the gabblings of others, can memorise a great deal of drivel, shoot off their horse-mouths and donkey-lips everywhere and swagger about.

Only the one who has awakened to the original condition of his being is a true master; only he has the ability to lead a student to Enlightenment. A fundamental principle of Zen is that no one can teach the truth of Zen as long as he has yet to awaken to the reality of his true being himself. My Master Soji Enku often used to say:

> Whoever presumes to talk about Enlightenment without being enlightened himself is like a man born without sight attempting to describe Michelangelo's ceiling painting of the Sistine Chapel.

Some of you might now be thinking: "Well if there are really so few real masters, then most people must be hopelessly lost in the sea of suffering of birth and death." We should not forget, however, that there are many upayas. These are preparatory teachings that may also be taught by guiding, unenlightened spiritual teachers. These teachers can at least bring students as far as they have come themselves.

But strictly speaking, the whole situation is nothing more than a tragic joke. It is like a swimming teacher who is himself a nonswimmer, and in trying to teach his pupils to swim sinks through the water like a stone. To this Lao-tse says:

> He who overly seeks honour,
> remains without honour.
> Do not wish to shine like a jewel,
> but then to fall like a stone.

Zen without Enlightenment is no more than a car without wheels. You can run the engine, and when you press the accelerator you can hear the strong engine. You can switch on the indicator, automatically open and close the windows, and much more. But there is one thing you cannot do and that is to drive! Yet that is the whole point, the whole raison d'être of a car. A car is a vehicle and a vehicle which you cannot drive is completely pointless.

Zen is the path to Enlightenment, and strictly speaking, a Zen teacher who purports he can lead others to Enlightenment is no more than a deplorable caricature.

There is "no Zen without Enlightenment"! Teaching the path to Enlightenment without being enlightened oneself is completely absurd and on top of everything also very dangerous. Jesus too said of this:

> If the blind lead the blind,
> both shall fall into the ditch.

Just as a real teacher is a great blessing for the student, so is a bogus teacher a great danger and hindrance.

What a responsible and reputable Zen instructor can really do, is to introduce the student to the practise of Zen meditation. He should impart to him the theoretical basis of the Zen teachings and foster the ethical side of his character. If he has been authorised by a true Zen Master – which can only be someone who has achieved Enlightenment – with a clear conscience he can call himself a Zen instructor. However, he should never presume to call himself "Zen Master".

Nowadays, one hears everywhere of spiritual teachers who appear as "authorised Zen teachers" and speak with assuaging words of Enlightenment, without having truly experienced it themselves. But what should one make of such blind moles who sit in their dark burrows and speak of the radiating light of the sun.

If a Zen teacher is honest enough he can lead a student a certain stretch of the way, but without the arrogating pretension of being able to lead him to Enlightenment. Furthermore, he must not tie the student to himself. Instead, he should lead the student far enough that he is ripe for a truly enlightened master. This should be his highest concern! Indeed, it is the whole purpose of a Zen teacher.

However, there are only very few people who are really ripe for the encounter with a master. Many people have encountered a master and then turned away because they did not recognise that a true master, an enlightened one, stood before them. This is the way it is today and that is how it has always been, right back to the times of Christ and Buddha.

Many people saw Buddha and turned their backs on him; they heard his wonderful teachings and said: "What rubbish". Many heard Jesus and said: "Who is that egomaniac who says he's the son of God? He must be a bit touched in the head. He is heavy with sweet wine and speaks deliriously. That is blasphemy, that cannot be a true master."

Many seekers come to a master with a preconceived notion – of a perfectly divine being, enshrouded by incense. When the master does not then correspond to their notions, and on the outside appears to be completely normal, they turn away from him, bitterly disappointed. Ultimately, since the master does not correspond to their conditioned notions, they deny that he is a master at all.

Yet, it is a fact that only a genuine, mature student finds the real, true master. In other words: whoever is unable to find a true master is not yet ready for a true master.

The question of what a true master is, to whom one can entrust oneself, cannot be answered without simultaneously reconsidering one's own qualification as student. In the end this means that when you seek a master then try to become a true student. If you do not meet the requirements for being a true student, how do you hope to find a true master?

You must truly be ripe for a genuine master. In the words of Meister Eckhart:

Friend, climb higher!

Then you surpass the false prophets, or "double-tongue masters", as they are called in Zen, until finally you find your personal master who leads you.

We now return to the starting point of our examination. All philosophical and religious systems are just relative aids and have as little to do with reality itself as does the finger with the moon to which it points. All cerebral acrobatic speculation has absolutely nothing to do with reality. Nothing at all!

What is it then? What is then the truth? A logical question. The intellect always thinks logically, and the answer it finds can only be logical too. Yet simply by being logical, the answer is wrong in the eyes of Zen, for "all conceptual thought is erroneous belief".

I would like to elucidate the absurdity of logic by means of a story:

One day, two lunatics in a mental home decide to break out.

The first one climbs down into the yard and quickly hides in the bushes.

But the warder hears a faint sound and calls: "Is anyone there?" On hearing a soft "miaow" from out of the bush, he says to himself reassured, "Oh, it's just a cat."

Now it is the turn of the other lunatic. Carefully he climbs down and jumps hastily into the bushes.

But the bushes sway back and forth so loudly that the warder is now very disquieted. In a loud voice he calls out: "Is anyone there?"

From out of the bushes comes the reply: "Another cat."

That is logic. The second lunatic had acted quite correctly according to the laws of logic. And since non-doubting words and notions is a terrible malady, we can spare ourselves the effort of delving more closely into the story.

Anything that can be conceptually expressed has nothing at all to do with the inexpressible reality which lies beyond everything that sense and reason can comprehend. The intellect thinks solely in terms of pairs of opposing concepts and says: If it is not this, then it is that. If it is not yang it must be yin, and if it is not yin, it must be yang. Or furthermore: If it is not movement, then consequently it must be stillness. But since it is neither this nor that, Buddha says of the absolute:

> One cannot say that it is, and one cannot say that it is not. One cannot say that it is and is not, and one also cannot say that it neither is nor is not.

This is the fourfold Buddhist negation. Zen Master Mumon expresses it in his own genial way. In his Gatha of Enlightenment he obliterates everything, so that finally, only MU – "nothing" – remains:

MU MU MU MU MU
MU MU MU MU MU
MU MU MU MU MU
MU MU MU MU MU

Nothing is real, nothing exists – for everything is just a dream without the slightest reality. Yet still you cling to the notion that behind this nothing is something – a thinker who thinks, sees, hears, feels, and understands. Yet precisely due to your clinging to this conditioned delusion you obscure the true, silent observer behind all experiences, your true self, without you even noticing it.

You believe that what you now perceive is your true self, but it is only the ego. For the ego which has been brought about by thoughts and the intellect is not a being, a person, but rather it is an occurrence – a process. It is an unrestrained process of identification and grasping. That is why in Buddhism it is known as Ahamkara, the process of ego-projection, the ego-maker, the I-delusion.

Many adherents to the esoteric scene – often "psychology gurus" – speak of having to kill one's ego. But this is utter nonsense since in truth, no ego exists, there is no ego you can kill. The sole thing you could and should kill is the delusion of an ego. And you can only kill this by putting an end to the process that sustains the ego-delusion. And what is this process? This process is that of constant, perpetual accepting and rejecting – the process of discrimination.

According to biblical tradition, this process had already begun in the Garden of Eden. God said that man should not eat of the tree of knowledge – of discrimination between good and evil – or he would be expelled from paradise. And so it has indeed happened, which is why you are sitting here right now.

In truth, though, you are still in paradise. Nothing has happened at all. It is just that the veil of acceptance and rejection has been draped over the pure perception of suchness, and now you can only see the projection of your ignorance and say, "This is how I am and this is how the world is." That is why Huang-po says:

> When thoughts arise, all things arise and when thoughts disappear all things disappear. When thoughts arise, all problems arise and when thoughts disappear all problems disappear.

Imagine you have a problem – any problem, no matter what – and you cannot free yourself from it. Then suppose that suddenly, while you are brooding over it, you are shot in the leg, and you now have a bullet lodged there. Are you still thinking about your problem? Just as a dog loves to chew on its bone, the intellect loves to bite into problems. You are convinced of being master of your intellect. But this is a great fallacy. It is not you who uses the intellect but the intellect that uses you.

You are so identified with your intellect that you have made yourselves its slave. But the intellect loses its power over you when you cease to identify yourselves with it. With this clear, non-identifying perspective you free yourselves from unrestrained compulsive thought. In the words of the Chinese Zen Master Fo-yan:

> Zen practise requires that you make yourself independent of thought. This is the best way of saving energy.
> Simply let go of all thought caused by feelings, and see clearly that there is no objective world. Then you will know how to practise Zen.

Zen Master Pai-chang, the master of Huang-po, gives us this wonderful instruction:

> When your mind moves do not follow it and it will detach itself from the movement. And when your mind rests on something do not follow it and it will detach itself from that on which it rests.

If you really want to enter the realm of Enlightenment it is essential to make your mind clear so that it is empty like empty space. Detach yourselves from old viewpoints and from all grasping!

Smash all your limitations! Stop trying to understand reality through the use of conceptual thinking, and your false ideas and suppositions will dissolve of themselves!

Free yourselves of everything and you are standing in the boundless Freedom of Zen! If you follow these instructions, you are truly on the path to Enlightenment.

14

The Original State Of The Mind

When a person's own mind recalls the original condition of his mind, all deceptive thoughts melt away by themselves in the realm of ultimate reality. There is no longer anyone who causes suffering and no one who suffers.
MILAREPA (TWELFTH CENTURY)

These words of one of the most significant masters of Tibetan Buddhism make very clear that one's own mind does not necessarily abide in the direct experience of its Self-Being, its original condition. And yet, the own mind is never separate from its original condition – from this One Mind which it is itself, and besides which nothing else exists.

Now imagine you point a straw up at the sky and look through the end of it. The boundless expanse of the sky is now reduced to a small point within this limited field of vision.

With the fixation of your restricting, dualistic thinking your perception thus becomes narrowed to a microcosmic partial aspect of the cosmic Mind. So there you are in a sorry state of contracted consciousness, with the illusion of an apparent individuality which experiences itself as separate from everything it perceives.

That which you generally term as "I" has no reality of itself. It is merely a fleeting combination of constantly changing energies. Your so-called individual existence is in truth nothing more than an uninterrupted, successive process of co-acting impersonal elements of existence. These elements of existence, the skandas, are divided in Buddhism into five groups. They are listed in order of decreasing density and materiality: corporeality, sensations, perceptions, mental formations, and consciousness.

However, none of these skandas, nor the skandas as a whole may be viewed as an autonomous self, existing of itself, not even consciousness, which in its fineness comes closest to the notion of a soul.

Consciousness should not be viewed here as an unchanging existence behind all experience, as many people believe, but rather as formations of consciousness – successive consciousness events. Consciousness is a "process of consciousness". It is not some reality underlying your experiences, but rather, consciousness is occurrence – a chain of successive consciousness moments.

Buddhist psychology describes this as "flashes of consciousness". These give rise to the illusion of a continuous, uninterrupted consciousness. It is comparable to a sequence of pictures on film that, when projected onto a screen, create the illusion of objects and movements.

For example, we are looking at a river, but what we really see is just a sequence of hundreds of images of moments of consciousness; and that means: it is no more than a chain of moments of existence and combinations thereof.

The individual moments of all the processes of spiritual and physical life are constantly changing, without interruption. They change so rapidly that this change cannot be perceived. Consequently, there exists nothing but a series of moments of existence and combinations thereof in the form of flashes of consciousness, each one following the other in quick succession.

All the elements of existence belonging to an individual and to the world of phenomena he experiences last no more than a brief instant – and a moment later there is already nothing left of what just came into being.

All the elements of existence which form the delusion of a personality are unstable and in actual fact have no being. They are merely appearance; they are merely occurrence, and have no independent existence whatsoever. For everything that comes into being is dependent on something which has gone before. Nothing is an entity unto itself, of itself. It is all occurrence in the form of illusion of phenomenon, dependent on what has gone before.

Everything which can form the contents of your perception arises in relationship to something else, and thus has a beginning. However; everything that has a beginning is governed by the law of coming into being and fading away, and will therefore also have an end. Yet beginning and end are illusory moments. They exist within a moment in time – but space and time have no reality.

Space and time are no more than categories of consciousness, that is to say, they are given conditions by which the individual consciousness perceives an apparent external world. In truth, however, it is all just conception or "idea", and thus being, not existing of itself.

Let us not delve too deeply now into the Buddhist psychology of perception, otherwise your heads might start to spin and the talk will become too long. The essential thing for you to know and understand is that the world as you perceive it is only a projection. It is a projection of consciousness – which is not something of its own being either, but rather – it is occurrence. Therefore, all perceptions, notions, and thoughts are not distinct from the thinker because all thoughts are illusory, as is the thinker who thinks them. Consequently, the thinker, too, is just an event – he has no real being. Let us now return to Milarepa's statement:

> *When a person's own mind recalls the original condition of his mind ...*

The original condition of your mind is the reality behind all experience. It is the One Mind, besides which nothing else exists and which remains completely unaffected by all forms of change and by death. In their essence, the One Mind and your own mind are one and the same reality. Therefore, to perceive the nature of your own mind means to perceive the nature of the all-embracing entirety of being. The One Mind is like the screen behind all pictures, movements, colours, and forms of a motion picture. When you perceive this impartial observer of all experiences, you perceive the original state of the Mind, and:

> *... all deceptive thoughts melt away by themselves in the realm of ultimate reality.*

"The deceptive thoughts" are the entire ego process: the process of consolidating and sustaining the illusion of an apparent personality, and thus the circle of birth, ageing, despair, illness, pain, and death. In other words, the impersonal elements of existence and samsara are one and the same process.

However, the own mind is never separate from the reality of the One Mind, whether it is aware of this or not. The moment the limitations of the individual mind fall, contracted consciousness, which is pseudo-individuality with its perceived world, dissolves away.

In this experience of emptiness – as vast and as open as the sky – the boundless expanse of the One Mind reveals itself, where previously it had enclosed itself within a self-made boundary and identified itself with this boundary. This Enlightenment experience can be likened to when a soap bubble bursts. The bubble's inner space and the space outside it dissolve into one another and become one.

Yet, this total liberation of the mind is not something you can willfully "do". You cannot force it. You cannot fight against your self-made limitation because the more you fight it, the more it solidifies into an insurmountable darksome dungeon. You imprison yourself in a prison of ignorance.

Let us now continue with the quotation from Milarepa, for the sentence continues:

When a person's own mind recalls the original condition of his mind, all deceptive thoughts melt away by themselves in the realm of ultimate reality. There is no longer anyone who causes suffering and no one who suffers.

"When thoughts arise, then do all things arise", says Huang-po, "and when thoughts vanish, then do all things vanish." And when all things vanish, so too do all the elements of existence which form the delusion of a personality, and thus the entire samsara vanishes. Everything vanishes which constitutes a pseudo-individuality in all its entirety.

The ego – in other words: the delusion of an independent personality – dissolves, and thus there is no longer anyone who causes suffering. And when there is no longer anyone who causes suffering, there is no one who suffers either.

Suffering does not come from the outside – it always comes from within. For the transitory nature of all pleasant things which you experience in the world can never cause you to suffer if you do not cling to them. That is why Meister Eckhart says:

> All suffering comes from love and affection. Thus, when I suffer on account of transitory things, then I and my heart have love and inclination for temporal things. So it is no wonder that God permits me to be rightly afflicted with loss and sorrow.

If you wish to cling to what is pleasant, or better still – what you believe to be pleasant – and then it is no longer there, suffering will always appear.

Yet the thing itself does not cause you to suffer. Suffering is brought on solely by attachment to transitory things. For attachment is hardening or stiffening, and hardening always means stagnation and non-movement. It is in opposition to the flow of Tao. That is why old Lao-tse says:

> The hard and rigid does not die a good death.

And Zen Master Yuan-wu says:

> All things become real in non-abiding. Let your mind flow, without lingering over anything. An ancient master says: "Let nothing bother you and do not linger over anything, be it from this world or not." If you linger, you come to a standstill and hinder your transformation.

And so, detach yourself from all your conditionings! Detach yourself from all your identifications with what you believe yourself to be and with what you once experienced! Free yourself from all intellectual refuse with which you have filled your brain! Free yourself from the shadows of a dead past, which are not worth losing even a single thought over, but nonetheless form the core of Western psychology.

If it weren't for rummaging around in this refuse, there would be no Western psychology, no therapy. This is the way of bridling the horse at the tail and only leads to going around in circles.

You can exert yourself as much as you like and can try using psychology to find a way out of your hopeless situation. You are bewildered and use all your might to attempt to escape, but you only entangle yourself ever more in the creeping snarl of your self-made spiritual confusion.

By so doing you remain caught in this spiritual chaos, in this blindness; in your prison of conditionings, behavioural patterns and thought patterns. It is even possible that you will wind up falling into a psychosis, or even worse, a permanent psychosis. And finally you end up in the madhouse.

Therefore, I give you this advice: Free yourselves of all this madness! But this is not something you can make happen. If, "now", in this instant, just as you are sitting before me, you let everything be just the way it is, and immerse yourselves in the immediate moment of Now, you recall your original state of the Mind.

This means that by forgetting yourselves and all things, you let go of everything and do not cling to the idea of a past and a future, which are no more than empty thoughts.

Past, present, and future are the consequence of the illusion of space and time, yet all this is like a leaf which is blown past the window of our consciousness by the autumn wind – and then it is gone.

Space and time constitute the samsaric core of how you experience the world. But a single instant in the immediate presence of pure awareness and you are in absolute "now", and the spectre of the "space-time illusion" dissolves away. Here, there is no I and no you, no coming and no going, no before and no after. Here, there is only "now", and this now is the reality of divine being of which Meister Eckhart says: "God is absolute now." You need not seek anywhere; you need not go anywhere.

Where would you seek the reality of your being that you yourself are? Where would you find the "divine light that shines in the darkness", to use the words of the prologue to the Gospel of John – where would you find it apart from in yourself?

Yet one thought and then another thought, and feelings and impressions have already begun to form. Then desire, hate, and blindness arise and samsara thus hardens all the more. All this obscures the true condition of the Mind, with the result that the divine light that shines in the darkness cannot be recognised.

Attempting to seek this light – your true being – by means of discriminating thought, by means of the intellect's capacity of perception would be just like wanting to find a candle, burning on a large open space in bright sunshine. It must be completely dark. "MU" – nothing! Nondesire, nonthinking. Finally having the courage to leave everything just as it is. This is the great faith which you must realise.

It is important to awaken this great faith within yourself. This takes place when, instead of relying on yourself, on your intellectual capabilities, you abide in wu-wei, in nondoing, and give the almighty being of the divine Universal Mind the chance to work. Wu-wei means: To abide in nondoing in such a way that Tao can work in you and through you. In the words of Meister Eckhart: "God works and I become."

You cannot force anything, for the simple reason that there is nothing to achieve. As soon as you believe there is something to achieve, some goal to reach, you find yourself in the hell of the demons of discriminating thought.

Yet these demons are none other than your own projections. They are your self-generated inner tensions that come from chasing after a wishful notion that only exists in your head, for inner tension is always impeded desire. "Now", everything is here! (Zensho stomps his staff on the floor!!!) You lack nothing at all. Not the least little thing. So what brings you to me? What is bothering you? Sons and daughters of the Highest, manifestations of divine reality. You are "absolute being, boundless consciousness, and infinite bliss", and all else is just bubbles, dreams and shadows, devoid of all reality. To this Milarepa says:

> *When a person's own mind recalls the original condition of his mind, all deceptive thoughts melt away by themselves in the realm of ultimate reality. There is no longer anyone who causes suffering and no one who suffers. The most exhaustive study of all holy scriptures teaches us no more than this.*

Recall the original condition of your Mind and never forget who you really are!

Do not identify yourselves with things you once experienced! Do not take yourselves to be what you once thought you were; how in your ignorance you saw yourselves, and how others saw you, or still see you! All that is no more real than a dream you once dreamt.

15

The Everyday Mind Is The Way

A student of Zen comes to Zen Master Nansen and asks him, "What is the way?"
The master replies, "The everyday Mind is the way."
The student asks, "How can one attain this everyday Mind?"
The master answers, "The more you seek it, the more you distance yourself from it."
The student then asks, "If I do not seek it, how can I know that it is the way?"
Master Nansen replies, "The way is not a matter of knowledge, nor is it a matter of ignorance. Knowledge is illusion, ignorance is indifferent non-awareness.
When you realise the way, your mind becomes as vast and as open as the sky, free of all limitations and boundaries. So how can one view the one as right and the other as wrong?"

"*What is the way?*" This is the question asked by the student Joshu, who himself later became one of the most significant masters of Zen. "What is the way?" means: What is the truth, what is the way of the buddhas? In other words: What is the way to Enlightenment? The master replies, "*The everyday Mind is the way.*" This statement by Zen Master Nansen is the foundation of Zen.

The everyday Mind of Zen is completely free and unpretentious. It makes no differentiation whatsoever between sacred and nonsacred, religious and nonreligious, spiritual and nonspiritual, right and wrong. It is nothing other than your ordinary, natural consciousness in your ordinary, normal life.

The everyday Mind is really very simple and nothing special: eating, drinking, sleeping, laughing, going for a walk – the flowers in the spring, the autumn moon. In the words of Zen Master Ma-tsu:

> The way requires no practise – just make sure you do not besmirch it. What is besmirchment? Having a labile mind which thinks up artificial measures and tricks – that is besmirchment.
> If you wish to directly experience the way, then ordinary consciousness is the way. By ordinary consciousness I mean mind which is without artificiality, without ego-oriented judgement, without attachment and rejection.

"The everyday Mind is the way", and it encompasses one's whole life. For the true way is Tao, which manifests itself in everything as the underlying reality of all things.

Everything is filled with the fullness of God. Everything is wonderful just as it is. Every discrimination is a dualistic viewpoint and a deviation from the reality of divine being. This is a thought we also find in the words of Meister Eckhart:

> A person may walk across a field and know God, or he may be in the church and know God.
> If he knows God more because he abides at a quiet place, then it is a result of his own inadequacy and no fault of God.
> For God is equally in all things and in all places

and is willing to give himself equally with his whole being.

In all things and in all places, in the midst of day-to-day life, it is essential that we experience the reality of our true being – everywhere, no matter where, right at the heart of everyday life. This is the everyday Mind, and "the everyday Mind is the way". The way and the goal are one, says Zen.

You need not go anywhere to find the highest truth. Tao lies beneath the soles of your feet. Stop projecting and entangling yourself in the creeping snarl of your discriminating, conceptual thinking! Open your eyes and be present! Be aware in everything that you do!

If you are truly aware in everything that you do the reality of your true being reveals itself to you – just as it is. Then, the whole world transforms for you into a radiant paradise with a wonderful collection of magnificently glowing fairy-tale flowers.

Most people believe the way to liberation is something extraordinary, and so they search for a very special way. They think, "Somewhere there must be the secret, the specific path, this particular golden thread – when we've found that, then we'll have it." Yet that is a big mistake.

You can search as long as you like – everything you find will be no more than the spawn of discriminating conceptual thought and completely worthless. No matter what colouration, what form of religion or philosophy it appears in, it cannot be reality.

The Zen student too from our example, who comes to Zen Master Nansen, believes the way to be something very special. And that is why he asks his master the question, "*What is the way?*" Yet Master Nansen's answer, "*The everyday Mind is the way*" immediately evokes in him the question, "*How can one attain this everyday Mind?*" He wishes to have a particular method, a system. He wishes something tangible which he can apply. But Zen Master Nansen gives him the astounding reply:

The more you seek it, the more you distance yourself from it.

This is a completely incomprehensible statement for common thinking and particularly for Western thinking. For the intellect it seems totally absurd and illogical, since in normal life the rule is: The more effort you put into something, the greater is your success. The more you learn, the more you know. The more knowledge you ingest on a subject, the more familiar you become with it and understand what it is about.

But take my word, you can read every single text ever written on Zen, and even memorise the lot, but you will not even have come one step closer to the truth of Zen. For the more you search for it, the more you are in danger of clinging to concepts and ideas. The more knowledge you amass through philosophical texts, the more you distance yourself from your inner reality.

Master Nansen's student has not yet understood the answer and so he goes on to ask, "*If I do not seek it, how can I know that it is the way?*" – And the Master says:

The way is not a matter of knowledge, nor is it a matter of ignorance.

A magnificent answer by one of the greatest Zen

Masters in the history of Zen. This answer contains the entire essence of Zen.

Tao, the way, is not a matter of knowledge nor is it a matter of ignorance. For in your imprisonment in logical dualism you believe: "If it is not a matter of knowledge then it must be something I cannot know." But Master Nansen swiftly sweeps this thought away too by adding, "... *nor is the way a matter of ignorance.*" It is neither one nor the other.

We cannot even say of Tao, the way, that it exists – that it has being. Neither can we say that it is pure nothingness. Huang-po therefore says of it:

> Tao exists, but in a way that is too wonderful for us to grasp. It is an existence which is no existence, a nonexistence which nonetheless exists. Thus this true void exists in a wonderful way.

The way has nothing to do with knowledge, nor has it anything to do with ignorance. For this reason Master Nansen says, "Knowledge is illusion. Ignorance is indifferent non-consciousness." However, this does not mean that it is entirely alright for you not to understand the true way.

If you take your ignorance for granted, you continue to live the mentally deranged life of an average earth-bound person. Like the majority of people, you eke out your miserable existence in indifferent non-consciousness.

If, on the other hand, you are convinced in all seriousness that you are capable of understanding Tao, the true way, then you are truly in a lamentable state of hopeless confusion. The true way is beyond knowledge and ignorance, and the everyday Mind is completely free of all acceptance and rejection. It is always just the way it is, with nothing to cloud it. It is open, clear, and pure.

When you realise the way, your mind becomes as vast and as open as the sky, free of all limitations and boundaries.

Yet do not interpret these words of Zen Master Nansen in such a way that you now think, "This is really a wonderful promise – but first I must achieve Enlightenment in order to experience it." If you think in this way you only confine yourself. You push experiencing your true being far into the future and thus miss the opportunity of the present moment. Be "now" here, and Tao is "now" reality.

The original condition of the Mind as your true being and the everyday Mind is one and the same reality. To experience it you need do no other than nondoing. Leave everything the way it is and open yourself completely to the present moment!

Be as vast and as open as the sky – not conditioned, not tense, not goal-oriented. Free yourself of your identification with the intellect which makes you a slave of discriminating conceptual thought! By identifying itself with the intellect, your unrestrained thought becomes compulsive, and thus you pointlessly squander your energy.

Compulsive thought is a terrible malady, an addiction. Freeing yourself of this addiction can only take place by being absolutely present in Here and Now. In this crystal clear consciousness, the everyday Mind is present in all things in the midst of daily life. It is entirely free of willful action and the notion of right and wrong. All of your everyday activities – be it eating, drinking, sitting, walking – are a revelation of the everyday Mind.

Regardless of where you are, regardless of what happens, you are as vast and as open as the sky, and thus you are transparent and lucid. You are beyond accepting and rejecting, and in the thick of the hustle and bustle of the world you abide in the cheerful serenity of the Mind.

In this instant – right here, where you are now – the everyday Mind reveals itself as the way. It is neither to be found in the past nor in the future.

"Here and Now" is reality, and everything else is a result of thought, and thus illusion. The everyday Mind is the way, and thus it is the way in the midst of everyday life. The truth of Zen reveals itself in the everyday Mind; it is very simple and nothing special. There is nothing special you need to attune yourself to.

> Once, another student came to Zen Master Nansen and asked him, "Did the sages of old have any secret teaching that I do not yet know?"
> "Yes", said Master Nansen.
> Eagerly, the student went on to ask, "What is this teaching?"
> The Master replied, "It is not the Mind, it is not Buddha, it is nothing at all."

In the words of Zen Master Nan-yueh, "Everything I could say of it would fall short of the mark." The highest truth cannot be expressed or described in words. And the reason for this is that the human language is very limited. It is not made to describe in words what lies beyond everything that sense and reason can comprehend.

Every attempt to describe the inexpressible reality within the confinements of limited human speech is completely pointless and only leads to confusion.

That is why Zen masters constantly strive to liberate their students from all intellectual refuse. With all available means, be it punches, blows with a stick, or ear-splitting roars, they strive to smash the disarray of intellectual concepts and explanations. Their aim is to lead the student to Enlightenment with uncompromising directness, as in the following example.

> Master Yun-men entered the Dharma hall and said: "Buddha achieved Enlightenment when the morning star appeared." To this a monk asked, "What is it like to achieve Enlightenment when the morning star appears?"
> The Master replied, "Come here and I'll show you!"
> The monk went up to him.
> The Master hit him with his staff and chased him out.

Another great Zen master was the Chinese Zen Master Ma-tsu of the Tang dynasty. His powerful teaching methods led many a student to Enlightenment. One of his most notable disciples was Pai-chang, who, triggered by Ma-tsu's hands-on teaching method, achieved Enlightenment:

> One day Pai-chang was with his master Ma-tsu in the garden behind the monastery when they saw

a flock of wild geese up in the sky. After the geese had flown off into the distance Ma-tsu asked, "What was that?"

"That was wild geese, Master."

"Where are they?" asked Ma-tsu.

"They have flown away, Master."

Ma-tsu suddenly grabbed Pai-chang's nose and twisted it so hard that, overcome with pain, he cried out loudly, "Ow, ow!"

"You say they have flown away", said Ma-tsu, "but how can it then be that they have all been here from the very beginning on?"

Sweat broke out from Pai-chang's every pore – he was enlightened on the spot.

A true Zen master is only ever interested in clarifying the student's mind so he can experience the original condition of his mind. This pure, empty mind is "your true face before your birth". This primal birthless and deathless reality prior to all being is constantly present, even if you do not experience it. It is not that it is sometimes more and sometimes less present. No; it remains unchangingly present – it is just that "you" are not present. In the words of Meister Eckhart:

> God is within, and you are without – this is in fact your whole problem.

If you would turn your whole energy inwards which you constantly squander by pointlessly brooding over what is, has been and how it was, and what could be, your true face before your birth would reveal itself. Then you would experience the eternal self-existing original essence of divine being as your true self. In the words of the Chinese Zen Master Huang-po:

> Then in an instant all the buddhas of all world systems will reveal themselves to you. You will recognise that the hordes of writhing and wriggling living beings are no more than shadows. Continents, as countless as grains of dust then appear to you to be no more than a single drop of the great ocean.
>
> The most profound teachings you have ever heard will be dreams and illusions to you. You will recognise all mind as the One Mind, and you will perceive all things as One.

16

Directly Grasping Reality

The One Mind alone is buddha, and there is no difference between buddha and sentient beings.
ZEN MASTER HUANG-PO (NINTH CENTURY)

"*The One Mind alone is buddha.*" The One Mind and the reality of your Self-Mind is one and the same reality. However, only very few believe that their own mind is buddha, the absolute. Most Zen students fail to take this seriously and thus live caught in their self-made bonds and compulsions.

All your systems of education and notions of belief condition you and make you crazy. You have become blind to the reality of your true self, to the point where you are no longer able to recognise who and what you are in truth.

All of your behavioural patterns and well-worn habitual thinking create an environment in which you have trapped yourselves and can no longer escape. In this situation of hopeless confusion let me ask you: What is the reality of your true being? Why do you not turn around and behold your original countenance before your birth?

The world you experience is only perceived because of duality. It is the reflection of your own consciousness. Without duality, no external world of phenomena exists either. The world is nothing more than a notion, a projection – it only exists in your consciousness.

You have trapped yourselves in your self-induced entanglement of discriminating conceptual thought.

You have turned yourselves into the goose in the bottle and have been taken in by the philosopher Ryoku.

> One day, the highly learned philosopher Ryoku goes to Zen Master Nansen and says:
> "There is a koan which has been bothering me for a long time. Can you please help me to solve the problem?"
> "Alright then, go ahead", says Master Nansen.
> Ryoku began: "Well, imagine that you have a large bottle with an opening just big enough for you to be able to lower a goose egg into it. After a time the egg hatches and a goose chick comes out. The chick grows bigger and bigger until one day there is a fully-grown goose in the bottle.
> Now I would like to ask you: how would you free the goose from the bottle without breaking the bottle or harming the goose?" Master Nansen remains silent for a moment ... Suddenly he calls out in a loud voice, "Ryoku!" such that the philosopher jumps back in shock – "Yes, Master?" – "Look, the goose is free!"

The philosopher had trapped himself so hopelessly in this whole mind-bending entanglement of discriminating conceptual thought that he had turned himself into the goose, and thus projected himself into his self-made bottle.

That is why, in Zen practise, you must recognise that the bottle – meaning your self-defined dualistic limitations – is merely a projection of discriminating, conceptual thought. Simply stop projecting and see things as they are!

In Zen it is a matter of seeing clearly and awakening to the point where you have completely awakened. As long as you are dreaming, you are in your dream – as the goose in the bottle. But when you awaken, there is neither goose nor bottle.

When, in easeful awareness of the Mind, you transcend your discriminating dualistic views, you will abide in natural clarity and achieve all-encompassing consciousness. In Zen this is called the realisation of "nondiscriminating clarity of the Mind".

The only thing that causes discrimination is this unbroken whirl of thoughts, notions and concepts, of feelings and conditionings in the form of behavioural patterns and thought models. All of this forms a thick veil over the radiating light of the Self-Mind.

For this reason, let me give you the following advice: Immerse yourselves "now" in Now! For if you do not do it now, when are you going to do it? Free yourself of everything!

Be truly here in this instant, without thoughts, without concepts, and without mental images! Free yourself of all concepts and do not cling to either past or future! Do not discriminate between Enlightenment and ignorance, or between life and death! Immerse yourself completely in this present moment! This is the path to direct, instantaneous perception of reality, just as it is.

Be without thoughts! For when thoughts arise, all things arise, and thus all problems; but when thoughts disappear, so do all things disappear, and thus all problems.

And so – no thoughts and no concepts! Simply be just the way you are – natural and spontaneous. But do not say, "So, now I am completely relaxed in Here and Now", because then you are once again tense and fixated, and once again you have a goal.

Mushotoku – without aim or striving for gain, as it is known in Zen. Immerse yourselves completely in the present moment – here-now – and do not cling to anything! Do not cling to silence either, such that noises from outside disturb you! When you hear a sound – then fully be this sound. Become yourself the sound of a passing car, become the singing of that bird, and the barking of that dog. Whatever it may be, it is all the One. The perceiver, the process of perception, and the perceived object – they are all one sole reality.

Everything is the One Mind, beside which nothing else exists. This is what you must recognise and immerse yourself in. Yet some of you may start to become afraid and then say, "If I am consistent in leaving everything behind me, immersing myself entirely in Now, who knows what could happen? It could happen that I suddenly experience such a change of awareness – a voidness of consciousness – that it draws me into a gaping abyss. Perhaps I will fall into such an emptiness that I will never come out of it again." Yet Chinese Zen Master Po-chan (seventeenth century) says of this:

> People should not worry whether they will be able to return to life again after mystical death. What they should be concerned with is whether they can die out of the state of being of "life"! The ancient masters used to say: "Bravely let go at the edge of the cliff. Resolutely and full of trust throw yourself into the abyss! Only after death do we begin to live. This alone is the truth."

The fear of letting go is nothing more than a result of your ignorance. You identify yourselves with the contents of your consciousness, and you are convinced that this is your reality.

Yet the moment when suddenly, the contents of your consciousness disappear, and for an instant you approach the border zone of the void of the Mind – in panic you immediately search for an anchor. You immediately cling tightly to your identifications which form the illusion of a personality.

You cling in panic-stricken fear because, in your ignorance, you believe that the individual elements of existence which form the illusion of a personality – corporeality, sensation, perception, mental formations, and consciousness – constitute your personality.

The fear of emptying the mind and falling into the void is what results when you cannot see through the deceptive nature of all phenomena and the attachment it leads to. However, when you suddenly realise that all phenomena, the entire universe, everything, whatever it may be is the indivisible One Mind, in the form in which it appears to you – what is left for you to fear?

This One Mind is the source of all life. It is the life which gives life to all life and therefore life itself. What does the water drop have left to fear when it falls into the great ocean and dissolves into it, thus experiencing itself as the endless ocean? Your fear of the void originates solely from the fact that you do not know that your own mind is the One Mind, and thus the void. Zen Master Huang-po says this too:

> You do not know that the instant you give up your conceptual thinking and forget your disquietude,

buddha will appear; for the Mind is buddha, and buddha is all sentient beings.

Your only problem is your fear of giving up conceptual thinking. It is the fear of the void; the fear of total annihilation.

You have a panic fear of death – and yet you are already dead! You are already dead because you have never immersed yourself in your true being, in the life that gives life to all life. You are already dead because, in truth, you are afraid of life. You have never immersed yourself in the life that reveals itself in the present moment of "Here and Now", and death approaches ever more. And that is why you are afraid.

However, your fear is nothing more than an empty emotion. "Where emotions arise, spiritual clarity is lost", says Lin-chi.

A true person of Zen has no fear of death. Since he has relinquished all knowledge and understanding, he abides in the all-encompassing abundance of life and lives from the wisdom of non-discriminating clarity of the Mind. The Chinese Zen Master Yuan-wu says this too:

> If you can relinquish your previous knowledge and understanding, if you leave open your heart and retain nothing in mind so that you experience a clear empty steadfastness, where speaking and thinking are no longer of significance, then you will fuse with the Essential, sink into the Eternal, and attain indwelling non-discriminating wisdom, which knows no attainment.

The wisdom of non-discriminating clarity is the reality of your Self-Being, it is the absolute "here", the absolute "now". It is the reality of your true being, which reveals itself now-here. It is the radiating light of the One Mind which illuminates the entire universe with its brilliance.

Truly having the courage to free yourself of everything, no matter what it is, is the way to Enlightenment. Throw away all opinions, all preferences, and dislikes! Even the smallest obstacle must be removed because the biggest is equal to the smallest and the smallest is equal to the biggest. A koan from the Mumonkan, a collection of koans from the thirteenth century tells us this too. It goes as follows:

> A cow goes through a window.
> Its head, its horns, its belly and its four legs are already through.
> How can it then be that the tail does not go through?

To make this very clear: the light of the One Mind shines forth only when everything that is blocking the light – however small, beautiful and sacred it is – has been swept out of the way. Zen Master Huang-po puts it as follows:

> The mind is filled with radiant clarity. So cast away the darkness of your old, dead concepts. Free yourselves of everything!

In other words: Let nothing – and whether it be so holy and full of philosophical wisdom – come between you and the direct, immediate experience of your true being!

Zen is the most free and most direct teaching, in which there is nothing to do and nothing to learn. It is the path which leads to directly and instantly grasping reality, just as it is.

Zen is a life without bonds, a life in freedom, and is freedom itself. Therefore, shatter your self-made chains of your grasping, inconsequential "I" — and your true self will shine resplendent in its entire grandeur, all-embracing and all-pervading!

Glossary

Advaita-Vedanta Skt. is one of the three major philosophical, theological systems in Hindu Vedanta. Its main leading exponent was Shankara (ninth century), one of India's greatest sages and philosophers. The Advaita-Vedanta teaches that the divine Universal Mind →Brahman, the Self →Atman and the external world of phenomena are utterly one. In Shankara's Viveka-Chudamani, "The Crest-jewel of Discrimination" it is written, "You are Brahman, pure consciousness, the observer of all experiences, and your true being is bliss."

Amida Jap. for →Amitabha (Skt.)

Amitabha Skt., "Boundless light", Jap. "Amida". One of the most important buddhas in →Mahayana Buddhism. It is the buddha of the "western paradise" →Sukhavati, not linked to a particular location but instead, indicating a state of consciousness of boundless light, of love and comprehension. According to the teachings of Shin-Buddhism, anyone who in deep faith calls Amitabha's name (especially at the hour of death), will be reborn in Sukhavati paradise. In the "Pure Land school", this call is known as Namu Amida Butsu, "worship of the buddha Amitabha." →Nembutsu.

Anitya Skt., literally: "impermanence, transitoriness". In Buddhism, one of the three characteristics of all conditional arising and thus all being. Everything that has arisen, dwells for a while and then decays once again – it arises, exists and decays. Impermanence is the fundamental law of the whole of existence. The two other characteristics are derived from this: "Nonsubstantiality (Anatman)" and "Suffering (Duhkha)".

Atman Skt., in Hinduism, the immortal true Self of mankind. As absolute consciousness it is the impartial observer behind all experiences and identical with →Brahman.

Avalokiteshvara Skt., "the lord who looks down upon all things, or who hears the cries of the world". He is the →Bodhisattva of compassion and embodies all-encompassing compassion (→Karuna) with all suffering beings. His byname is "Mahakaruna", great mercy, one of the main facets of a buddha. The other main facet of a buddha is wisdom (→Prajna), which is embodied in a special way by Bodhisattva →Manjushri. Avalokiteshvara's boundless compassion is seen in his constant readiness to help all those beings who turn to him in their suffering. In Tibet, Avalokiteshvara is revered as →Chenresi, in China as →Kuan-yin and in Japan as →Kannon (also Kwannon or Kanzeon).

Avatamsaka-Sutra Skt. →Hua-yen

Avidya Skt., literally: "ignorance, non-recognising". Avidya is seen as the root cause for the attachment to →samsara – the circle of birth and death. Ignorance is the root of all suffering, for it is that state of mind which is not in accordance with reality. In →Mahayana Buddhism, Avidya is denoted as non-recognition of the voidness (→Shunyata) of all things. Thus, non-recognition of the deceptive nature of all phenomena is the true reason for all suffering.

Bardo Tibet., literally: "intermediate state", relates to the intermediate state between death and reincarnation. Buddhist teaching strongly stresses the direction defining force of the state of mind of a dying person (meaning virtuous, not-virtuous or neutral) and also the negative influences of greed, hate and ignorance during bardo itself.

Beginner's mind →Shoshin

Bodhi Skt., literally: "Awakening, Enlightenment". →Satori

Bodhichitta Skt., "Spirit of Enlightenment", the endeavour to achieve Enlightenment for the good of all beings in order to free them from suffering. Also, the direct term for the enlightened Mind itself.

Bodhisattva Skt., literally: "Enlightenment-being". A person who, having reached Enlightenment (→Satori), spends his life in the service of others to help them reach liberation. The term Bodhisattva is often used to denote a future →buddha.

Brahman Skt., the one, eternal, all-pervading absolute, origin and bearer of the entire universe. The philosophy of Vedanta (→Advaita-Vedanta) teaches that Brahman; the Absolute, surpassing the personal level and →Atman; the true Self in all beings, are one. Brahman, the sole existing truth, is the essence and the Self (Atman) of all being. The Viveka-Chudamani, one of the most significant texts of Advaita-Vedanta, says: "Atman is one with Brahman. This is the highest truth: Only Brahman is real. There is nothing else besides it. When it has been recognised as highest reality, there exists nothing else besides Brahman." This insight that Brahman and Atman are one is regarded as the highest goal, since it brings liberation from the imprisonment in →samsara, the cycle of birth and death.

Buddha Skt., literally: "the awakened one". 1. The historical Buddha Shakyamuni, who was born in India in circa 563 B.C. 2. A person who has fulfilled complete Enlightenment (→satori), liberating him from the cycle of birth and death (→samsara). 3. The final truth, the true nature of all being.

Buddha-Dharma Skt. (Jap. Buppo), "buddha-law". The teachings of the historical Buddha Shakyamuni. In Zen, however, we do not denote buddha-dharma as a teaching that can be conveyed in words, rather it is the highest truth, inaccessible for discriminating, conceptual thinking. It is that essential truth which led to Buddha's teachings and which can only be conceived in direct comprehension, in the experience of Enlightenment (→satori).

Buddha-Nature Skt., "Buddhata", the true nature of all beings, which makes it possible for a person to reach Enlightenment (→satori).

Chakra Skt. →Kundalini

Chan Chin. for Zen (Jap.)

Chenresi Tibet., literally: "the lord who does not turn his face to suffering". The Tibetan form of →Boddhisattva's →Avalokiteshvara. The most often recited →mantra in Tibet, →OM MANI PADME HUM is dedicated to him.

Cycle of birth and death →samsara

Daigo-Tettei Jap., literally: "Great →Satori which reaches down to the ground". Highest complete Enlightenment. One of its principle characteristics is the experience of empty vastness and the lifting of all contrariety with the destruction of the small "I". Furthermore, the experience that the whole universe and the Self-Mind are completely identical.

Dharma Skt., a term with various meanings. The teachings of →Buddha. Universal order and its laws. In this book, mainly used in the sense of the teachings of →Zen.

Dharmakaya Skt., "Body of the great Order". The indescribable true being of the →buddhas, and at the same time, the essence of the universe.

Dorje Tibet., "Diamond". →Vajra

Dzogchen Tibet. →Mahamudra

Enlightenment →Satori

Great Death →Satori

Hara Jap., literally: "Belly, abdomen". This common →Zen term denotes the area approximately three finger widths below the belly button as the centre of all being. It is the centre of every person and at the same time the centre of the universe. Through the practise of →zazen and correct breathing a great energy and power develop in this centre. Hara, as the centre of energy, is in Zen the point of origin of all activity (as in the meaning of "acting on intuition", but in Zen its meaning goes much deeper).

Hinayana Skt., "small vehicle". Oldest school of the two main branches of Buddhism. The original derogatory term "small vehicle" originates from the exponents of the later school of →Mahayana Buddhism. The main endeavour of Hinayana Buddhists is to reach their own liberation from →samsara, the cycle of birth and death.
Here, little consideration is made for liberating other beings from the sea of suffering of samsara. In the rescue boat of the small vehicle there is only room for one person. Hinayana is viewed as the first step of Buddha's teachings. Only later did →Buddha reveal the complete teachings of Mahayana.

Hishiryo Jap., literally: "that which thinking cannot fathom" or also: thinking without thinking.

Ho! Chin., this powerful, loud cry is often used by Zen masters as an abrupt means of expression to shatter the fixated, discriminating thinking of the student.

Hua-yen Chin., (Jap. Kegon, Skt. Avatamsaka), literally:

"floral decorations" or "garland"; originally the name of a comprehensive →Mahayana text. The Hua-yen is seen by many Chinese and Japanese Buddhists as the crown of all Buddhist teachings and the perfection of Buddhist thought and realisation. Hua-yen is the doctrine of holistic being, and at the same time, a synthesis of all major Mahayana thinking. In Hua-yen, the universal One Mind is compared with the endless surface of the ocean, in which all things and events in mutual pervasion are an all-encompassing whole, which contains everything within itself. Everything is in perfect harmony together, for everything is the manifestation of the one principle – similar to the waves on the ocean. Everything in the universe, whether animate or not, is thus the One Mind, beside which nothing else exists.

Ishin-Denshin Jap., literally: "to transmit Mind by means of Mind". A fundamental concept of →Zen, often translated as "transmission of Mind to Mind". The term originates from the Platform Sutra by the sixth patriarch Hui-neng. In this →sutra, Hui-neng explains that the truth of Zen can only be realised through one's own experience, in a direct understanding of its true nature. Scholarliness gained through reading is worthless – thus Hui-neng's act of tearing apart the sutras. Zen Master Huang-po says: "There is no understanding through words, but merely a transmission from Mind to Mind."

Joriki Jap., the power of concentration gained through Zen meditation (→zazen).

Kannon, Kanzeon or also Kwannon, Jap. for →Bodhisattva →Avalokiteshvara.

Karma Skt., literally: "Action or deed". The law of cause and effect, by which all thoughts and actions have a corresponding consequence. Through this we determine the quality of our own lives and influence that of others.

Karuna Skt., literally: "compassion", all-embracing compassion. One of the principal virtues in →Mahayana Buddhism; the other being →Prajna. (→Avalokiteshvara)

Kensho Jap., seeing one's own nature. →Satori

Kinhin Jap., The practise of walking meditation, which is usually performed for ten to fifteen minutes between the individual →zazen periods of sitting. In traditional →Rinzai Zen the walking pace is quick and brisk, in →Soto Zen, on the other hand it is very slow. Some contemporary Zen masters often set a tempo which lies between these two forms.

Koan Jap., literally: "public notice" (Chin. Kungan). In Zen, the term for a paradox quote from a Zen master which points to the ultimate truth. A koan is used to aid a Zen student in overcoming discriminating dualistic thinking so that he reaches the truth beyond all thinking. Koans play an important role in Zen instruction. A koan contains a question for which there is no answer for the intellect. To solve it, a higher intuition (→Prajna) is required. However, a koan is everything but a puzzle since it requires the student to abandon his faith in his own, normal way of understanding. The answer lies beyond logic and it is there to aid the student to break through to the enlightened clarity of the Mind.

Kuan-yin Chin. for →Avalokiteshvara

Kundalini Skt., "Snake power". The spiritual energy in every person which rests in the Muladhara chakra at the lower end of the spine. When awakened, it rises up through the spine and pervades the individual chakras (centres of subtle, delicate energy), until it reaches the thousand-petalled lotus of the Sahasrara chakra directly above the top of the head. Ultimately, at this point, in the seventh centre, beyond the coarser material body, this cosmic energy unites with the Divine.

Lila Skt., literally: "Game". In Hinduism, Lila is the divine game in the world of phenomena. The whole of creation is described as God's game.

Mahamudra Skt., "Great symbol". The principle teaching of the Kagyu school of Tibetan →Vajrayana Buddhism. Mahamudra is also translated as the "great seal". This thus expresses the significance of finality, as with a seal. Similar to the practise of →Dzogchen in the Nyingma line, Mahamudra practise is about directly perceiving the light-nature of the Mind and thus reaching Enlightenment (→Satori).

Mahayana Skt., literally: "Great vehicle", as opposed to the earlier orthodox school of →"Hinayana". Mahayana Buddhism attaches a much greater importance to all-embracing compassion (→Karuna) and the wish to help all beings reach liberation than it does to abstinence. Mahayana also includes the helping power of the →buddhas and →bodhisattvas.

Mahayana-Buddhism, Mahayana teachings →Mahayana

Maitreya Skt. (Jap. Miroku), literally: "The all-loving one". One of the five earthly →buddhas, the embodiment of all-embracing love. The Mahayana Buddhists anticipate that this, the last earthly buddha, currently abiding in Tusita Heaven, will come as a teacher of the worlds in around thirty thousand years' time.

Maitri Skt., literally: "Goodness and mercy". One of the prime virtues in Buddhism. It is charitable goodness towards all beings, free from all attachments.

Maitri-Karuna literally: "Goodness and compassion". The fundamental state of mind of a →Bodhisattva, which is expressed in his desire to lead all beings to liberation.

Makyo Jap., approx. "devilish phenomena", deceptive, distracting phenomena and sensations which can arise during Zen meditation (→zazen). Makyos can appear in a variety of forms; as wonderful sounds, smells, faces, prophetic visions, sometimes also as levitation. However, Makyos are quite harmless as long as the zazen practitioner takes no heed of them and continues his practise unperturbed.

Manjushri Skt. (Jap. Monju), literally: "He who is noble and kindly". One of the most important →Bodhisattvas in →Mahayana Buddhism. Manjushri is the embodiment of wisdom. He is most commonly depicted with his sword of wisdom, cutting through ignorance. His raging Tantric appearance is that of the bull-headed Yamantaka, the vanquisher of death.

Mantra Skt., one or a series of syllables, filled with spiritual energy, which the student recites either verbally or in the mind. Constantly repeating a mantra leads to realisation of the true being by way of purification of the thoughts. However, a mantra is only endowed with transforming powers when one has received it directly from the master (→OM MANI PADME HUM).

Mara Skt., Pali, literally: "Murderer, destroyer (of life)". Mara is the personification of the obstacles on the road to liberation. As the tempter and the phenomenon of unwholesomeness, he can be compared with the Christian devil, the "Father of lies". His three daughters are seen as his helpers: rati – desire, avati – discontent, and tanha – greed. In addition, Mara is supported by a whole army of demons.

Maya Skt., literally: "Illusion, semblance, deception". In Vedanta philosophy (→Vedanta), Maya is the power of great illusion. It veils one's view so that one is unable to recognise →Brahman, ultimate reality. Shankara links Maya to →Avidya, ignorance. Ignorance, that is, nonperception of the ultimate reality of Brahman, creates the delusion of an external world of phenomena in space and time by means of its obscurement. →Mahayana

Buddhism characterises Maya as a deception or illusion, just like a phantasm created by a mirage. Individual things are provisory and have no existence of their own, they are in fact void (→Shunyata) and mere conception.

Ming-Dynasty Chinese epoch, 1368 – 1644

Mondo Jap., "question-answer" (Chin. "Wen-ta"), a dialogue between Zen Master and student, also often just between Masters. In answer to a question concerning Buddhist truth or an existential problem, the student normally receives a paradox (→Koan), which cannot be classified by the intellect. The aim behind this is to smash the bounds of discriminating, conceptual thinking so that the student can obtain an answer from his innermost intuition.
A very well-known Mondo is: A Zen monk asked Zen Master Joshu: "What is the meaning of the first patriarch's coming from the west?" Joshu said: "The cypress tree in the courtyard."

Mu Jap. (Chin. Wu), literally: "Nothing, non-being, is not, has not, un-, none". One of the central concepts of →Zen and →Taoism. It describes utter freedom from all identification and attachment, and also stands for realisation of the void (→Shunyata). In the well-known Koan collection of the Mumonkan we encounter "Mu" in the first example, "Joshu's dog". In Zen it is also known as "the →koan Mu". "A monk respectfully asked Master Joshu: 'Does a dog have Buddha-Nature or not?' Joshu answered: 'Mu'".

Mudra Skt., a special posture of the hands with symbolic meaning.

Mumonkan Jap., literally: "The gateless gate". Alongside the →Pi-yen-lu, the most important collection of koans in Zen Buddhism (→Zen). It contains a collection of 48 →koans, compiled by Zen Master Mumon (thirteenth century) and accompanied by short Zen explanations.

Mushin Jap. (Chin. Wu-hsin); "Non-thinking, seclusion of the mind". A natural state of mind entirely without aim, beyond all thought.

Nembutsu Jap. (Chin. Nien-fo), invocation of the name of →buddha →Amitabha. The western meditation form of the Buddhist school of the Pure Land (→Pure Land school). The invocation recited is "Namu Amida Butsu" (Jap. for "homage to the buddha Amitabha"). Nembutsu recited in complete faith and absolute devotion leads to reincarnation in Sukhavati, the western paradise of the buddha Amitabha.

Nirvana Skt., literally: "extinguishment". The state of complete liberation (→Enlightenment), as opposed to →samsara, imprisonment in the cycle of birth and death. The Zen Buddhist does not view nirvana as separate from the world but as a state of consciousness in which one fulfils one's true being and thus surpasses suffering.

OM ancient holy Indian symbol. It is one of the most important →mantras in →Tantric Buddhism, which is spread across the whole of the East. It stands for the all-encompassing, all-pervading presence of the Absolute in the universe. It is the divine original tone, which reflects the beginning and the essence of the entire cosmos as vibrations. (See also →mantra and →OM MANI PADME HUM)

OM MANI PADME HUM Skt., literally: "→OM, jewel (in the) lotus, HUM". Invocation form for the →Bodhisattva →Avalokiteshvara. In this →mantra, "OM" and "HUM" stand for the beginning and the end, and symbolise totality. The meaning of "Jewel in the lotus" comes from the sameness of the jewel and the Spirit of Enlightenment (→Bodhichitta), with the wish to awaken it in the lotus of the consciousness. The Tibetans repeat this mantra constantly in order to strengthen their own devotion and affinity with Avalokiteshvara, the Bodhisattva of compassion.

Pi-yen-lu Chin., literally: "Blue Cliff Record", Jap. Hekigan-roku. The most important collection of koans in Zen Buddhism (→Zen) alongside the →Mumonkan. It was published in the twelfth century by the Chinese Zen Master Yuan-wu, one of the most significant masters in the history of Zen. It involves a collection of 100 →koans which, together with additional texts, belong to the zenith of the whole of Zen literature.

Prajna Skt., literally: "Wisdom" (Pali: Panna, Jap. Hannya). In →Mahayana Buddhism Prajna is intuitively experienced insight into the voidness (→Shunyata) of all phenomena. Prajna is one of the principle characteristics of Buddhahood.

Pratitya-Samutpada Skt., literally: "Emergence in mutual conditionality and dependence". The doctrine of the chain of conditional emergence is the foundation of all Buddhist schools. A deeper understanding of Buddhism depends on one's grasp of this doctrine.

The Pratitya-Samutpada shows that all phenomena have no more than an empirical validity and are thus devoid of reality. All phenomena exist respectively in a causal and conditional relationship of dependence on each other and to each other. Nothing is to be found which is nondependent and which has an existence out of itself.

Pure Land (Chin. Ching-tu, Jap. Jodo) →Sukhavati

Pure Land School →Amitabha

Rinzai School (Chin. Lin-chi-tsung, Jap. Rinzai-shu). Alongside the →Soto school, one of the predominant schools of Zen Buddhism (→Zen) in Japan. The striking feature of Rinzai is the systematic use of →koans for gaining Enlightenment (→Satori).

Roshi Jap., literally: "old, venerable master". Originally, the title of a Zen master. In times of old a Zen monk could only gain this title with great difficulty. It was only bestowed on those who had been acknowledged as having fulfilled →buddha dharma by way of directly experiencing it, and who were able to carry it over into everyday life. Total Enlightenment (→Satori) and a mature personality with a steadfast character were the necessary prerequisites.

Today, true, completely enlightened Zen masters in Japan are extremely rare. The term "Roshi" has now been reduced to a general title for a Zen teacher, regardless of whether monk or layman. In respect of their age and position, monks are often addressed as "Roshi", so that this term is now empty and meaningless.

Samadhi Skt. (Jap. Sanmai or Zanmai), literally: "to fasten, to fix". A state of non-intentionality and freedom from thoughts. It is the state of being focussed on a single object, brought about by calming the activity of the mind. In this non-dualistic state of consciousness the person meditating and the object of meditation become completely one. All dualism and the belief in a self, existing of itself and separate from everything else are overcome in Samadhi. However, this state of consciousness of Samadhi, free of all thinking, is neither stuporous nor unfeeling. Quite the contrary, it is the crystal-clear awareness of the Mind. A person immersed in Samadhi experiences an intensive feeling of inspiritment of a psychic-physical nature, which is immeasurably greater than everything that he has previously experienced.

Samsara Skt., literally: "roaming". The cycle of birth and death. The aim of all Buddhists and Hinduists is liberation from samsara, and thus from suffering. It is liberation from the imprisonment in the wheel of birth, ageing, despair, illness, pain and death.

Sat-Chit-Ananda Skt., literally: "Being (Sat), consciousness (Chit), bliss (Ananda)". In →Vedanta, this term represents the experience gained through Enlightenment of the inexpressible truth of the Absolute, →Brahman, as absolute being, boundless consciousness and bliss.

Satori Jap. (Chin. Wu), Zen term for the experience of Enlightenment, or awakening. Satori is far more than an intuitive understanding of true Being, as in the experience of →Kensho, since the person who experiences Satori dissolves entirely into it. In →Zen, Satori is described as the rebirth of the true Self once the false, illusory self, the ego-delusion has died the "Great Death".

Sesshin Jap., literally: "Concentration of the Mind (Hsin)". Intensive →Zazen sitting periods lasting several days in total, interspersed with speeches by the master and the opportunity of a one-to-one talk (Dokusan).

Shastra Skt., literally "textbook, instruction".

Shikantaza Jap., "Just sitting" →Soto school

Shoshin Jap., "Beginner's mind". The necessary state of mind of a Zen student for Zen instruction by a master. It is the attitude of mind in which the student recognises that he knows nothing. It is the absolute prerequisite for letting go of everything that sense and reason can comprehend.

Shunyata Skt. (Jap. Ku), literally: "emptiness, void". According to the teachings of Mahayana nothing possesses a self-dependent, lasting substance. All things are empty and thus without self-nature. The teaching of shunyata is one of the cornerstones of the whole of →Mahayana Buddhism and accordingly of →Zen. It is very subtle and cannot be expressed in words. Although there is extensive literature covering this subject, shunyata is only completely understandable for those who have experienced it themselves in the experience of Enlightenment (→Satori).

Skandha Skt. (Pali: Khandha), "group, amassment". In Buddhism, the five groups which constitute and define the human personality as it is commonly known.
Corporeality group (Rupa)
Sensation group (Vedana)
Perception group (Samjna)
Mental formations, psychic forming force (Samakara)
Consciousness (Vijnana)
What we commonly view as being our personality is in truth nothing more than a mere process of these psychic-physical phenomena.

Soto School (Chin. Tsao-tung-tsung, Jap. Soto-shu). Alongside the →Rinzai school, one of the two principle schools of Zen Buddhism (→Zen) in Japan. As opposed to Rinzai, Soto does not make use of →koans but rather, it practises a form of Zen comprised exclusively of just-sitting →Shikantaza, literally: "nothing but sitting". Since it insists on putting zazen on a par with Enlightenment (→Satori), Soto is known as "silent Enlightenment Zen".

Spirit of Enlightenment →Bodhichitta

Sukhavati Skt., "blissful", the western paradise, ruled by →buddha →Amitabha. Reincarnation in Sukhavati paradise has the effect that one can no longer fall back into a reincarnation in other realms (→Nembutsu).

Sung-Dynasty Chinese epoch, 960-1278

Sutra Skt., literally "guideline". Sutras are the most important texts in Buddhism. Most of the sutras are instructive talks by →Buddha. In →Mahayana Buddhism many additional sutras were later written and are regarded as being authoritative. They emerged between the first century B.C. and the sixth century A.D.

Tang-Dynasty Chinese epoch, 618-906; the period in which Zen Buddhism was at its peak. (→Zen)

Tantrayana →Vajrayana

Tantric Buddhism →Vajrayana

Tao Chin., literally: "Way", central metaphysical term of →Taoism. Tao is the Absolute, the fundamental all-encompassing principle; the ultimate truth. Tao forms the core of Lao-tse's →Tao Te King and the teachings of Chuang-tse. The aim of all Taoists is to live in unison with Tao. Intellectual understanding is not enough, instead it is a matter of fulfilling the unity, simplicity and →voidness of Tao. "Action without intent", →Wu-wei, literally: Non-action, is seen as the principal attitude of mind of a Taoist.

Taoism There are two main streams of Taoism – the philosophical stream: Tao-chia, and the religious stream: Tao-chiao. Tao-chia dates back to the Taoist master Lao-tse and his book, the →Tao Te King. Here, acting without intent in unison with →Tao is seen as the highest ideal. On the other hand, the aim of the religious

Taoism is physical immortality. It is to be achieved through breathing exercises, physical exercises and certain sexual practices.

Tao Te King Chin., literally: "The book of Tao and true virtue". A work from the sixth century B.C. ascribed to the old Taoist master Lao-tse. It comprises five thousand characters and is therefore also known as "the book of the five thousand characters". The Tao Te King is the cornerstone of →Taoism and at the same time one of the most important and most translated books of world literature. The author of the Tao Te King must seem concealed and mysterious to us, just like the Tao of which he speaks. Lao-tse is said to have reached a very old age of well over a hundred years. He lived in Tschou, but as he saw that it was in the process of decaying he departed. On arriving at the border pass he encountered the border guard Yin Hsi, who recognised the master and begged him to leave behind something in writing. Thereupon, Lao-Tse wrote his book, the Tao Te King in which he expressed his thoughts on Tao and true virtue. Subsequently, riding on his buffalo, he departed. No one knows what became of him.

Tathata Skt., "Thusness, thus-being, that which is". A core concept of →Mahayana Buddhism. It describes the Absolute, the true nature of all things. Tathata is beyond all dualistic concepts, it is unchanging and the opposite of the semblance of phenomena. As the thusness of all things it is formless, uncreated and without self-nature. It is identical to →buddha-nature and thus equivalent to the →dharmakaya.

Tathagata Skt., literally: "The one who has thus gone (thus arrived there, thus-come)". This term is meant as an honorary title to express Buddha's identity as a consummate being. As a perfectly enlightened →buddha he acts as a mediator between the Absolute and the world of phenomena.

Te Chin., literally: "virtue, power". The acting force of the →Tao, as revealed to those who live in unison with the Tao. Lao-Tse calls "Te" true virtue in his Tao Te King. It is what can be called spontaneous experience through Tao. Although Te is generally translated as virtue, it should not be overlooked that it has nothing to do with the conventional term for virtue as it is commonly known. Te is not the virtue of moral rectitude, which, by clinging to external moral codes degenerates into a virtue-conscious mentality, to which Lao-Tse says: High virtue is not virtue-conscious, therefore it is true virtue. Lesser virtue is virtue-conscious, therefore it is not true virtue. (Verse 38) Real, true virtue emanates from an inner balance, to be understood as an inner force. It is the radiating and merciful power of the Tao, which acts on the surroundings of the wise one, rooted in Tao as pleasant, spontaneous goodness.

Thanka Skt., iconographic picture. In →Tibetan Buddhism it is a scroll painting, painted on fabric and edged with silk. It fulfils various religious functions.

Tibetan Buddhism →Vajrayana

Upanishads Skt.: Upanishad, literally: "to sit close by", i.e. to sit near to the master to receive the secret teachings. The Upanishads are a category of texts which make up the final part of the Veda and are the fundamental basis of →Advaita-Vedanta. They are concerned with ultimate truth and belong to the holy revelation scriptures of Hinduism.

Vajra Skt. (Tib.: Dorje); "diamond", diamond sceptre. Symbol for the indestructibility of the void (→Shunyata), as the true Being and the essence of all that is.

Vajrayana Skt., literally: "diamond vehicle", often known as Tantric Buddhism, also as Tibetan Buddhism. In Vajrayana, the practitioner works creatively with the force of imagination given to him by his Master. This takes place through use of visualisation and →mantras, by identifying himself with his →Yidam, a special pictorial manifestation of a →buddha. For this reason, Buddha statues, Mandalas, and Thankas (iconographic representations) play a large role as a memory aid for visualisation in Tantric Buddhism.

Vajrayana-Buddhism →Vajrayana

Vedanta Skt. →Advaita-Vedanta

Void, voidness, emptiness →Shunyata

Wu Chin., literally: "Nothing, non-being" →Mu

Wu-hsin Chin. →Mushin

Wu-wei Chin., literally: "Non-action" in the sense of "action without acting". This Taoist term is not to be confused with passively doing nothing. Much rather, it means the attitude of mind of non-intervention in the natural course of things. In truth, Wu-wei is a highly effective state of mind, in which any action is possible at any time. By living non-action, the Taoist sage is in unison with Tao, whose universal power is brought to bear exactly due to this non-action. The great Taoist master of old, Lao-tse, says in his →Tao Te King: Tao is eternally without action, but nothing remains undone. Wu-Wei is a matter of creative non-action, an actless conduct which underlies the mental attitude of non-intervention and the courage of letting things happen. Wu-Wei transcends both extremes – restless activity and absolute inactivity. It is a non-action of the unimportant, which at the same time allows the essential to take effect.

Yamantaka Skt. →Manjushri

Yidam Skt. →Vajrayana

Zanmai Jap. →Samadhi

Zazen Jap., literally: "sitting in immersion", (Chin. Tsao-chan). Common meditation practise in →Zen. All great masters of Zen view zazen as a practise which is indispensable and fundamental in Zen. Zazen means abiding of the Mind in a state of crystal-clear awareness, free of content and not focussed on any object.

Zen Jap., an abbreviation of "Zenna", the Japanese way of reading the Chinese "channa" (in short, chan), which itself is a transcript of the Sanskrit word "Dhyana".

Zen-Buddhism developed in the 6th and 7th centuries in China from the combination of Bodhidarma's transmission of Indian Dhyana-Buddhism and Chinese Taoism. Characteristic of Zen is its particularly strong emphasis on the experience of Enlightenment (→Satori). Integral to Zen is also the development of intuitive comprehension through meditation (→zazen) instead of intellectual studies. The fundamental characteristics of Zen were summarized in the early →Tang-Dynasty in four short sentences in Chinese:

1. Transmission outside the orthodox teachings
2. Independence from holy scriptures
3. Directly pointing towards the Mind (Hsin)
4. Perception of one's own nature and attainment of Buddhahood

Zen-Buddhism →Zen

Contact

ZEN-ZENTRUM
TAO 道禪 CHAN

Tao Chan Zentrum e.V.
Yorckstraße 6
D-65195 Wiesbaden
Germany

The Tao Chan Zen Centre is under the personal direction of Zen-Master Zensho W. Kopp.
During his many years as an active spiritual master, a large community of students have come together whom he regularly instructs.

Zen-Weekend
Once a month, Zen Master Zensho leads a two-day Zen-weekend where those interested may participate.

Information and registration
Tel. +49 (0)611 940 623 -1 Fax -2
E-Mail info@tao-chan.de
www.tao-chan.de

ZENSHO W. KOPP

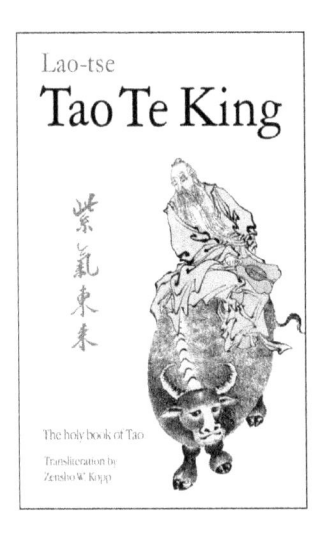

Lao-tse, Tao Te King
The holy book of Tao

Transliteration
by Zensho W. Kopp

110 pages, paperback
Print on Demand
Available at www.tao-chan.de

The 2500 year old Tao Te King by the Chinese sage Lao-Tse is a jewel of Eastern wisdom. It counts as one of the most profound and most translated books of world literature.

In a language of incomparable imagery the Tao Te King speaks of the Tao, the divine origin of all existence, and its effect on man as true virtue. Its goal is to lead him back to the original oneness with the Tao, and so into harmony with the all-embracing wholeness of existence.

In this outstanding new transcription, Zensho has succeeded in masterly conveying the whole mystical expressiveness of the work whilst strictly adhering to the original sense, and thus providing a completely new and deeper insight.

A timeless book of wisdom, unique mysteriousness, and linguistic beauty.

ZENSHO W. KOPP
BOOKS IN GERMAN

Zen-Worte der blitzartigen Erleuchtung

Mit umfangreicher Koan und Mondosammlung

320 Seiten, 17,95 €
ISBN 978-3-89767-915-3
Hardcover
Schirner Verlag

100 Juwelen der Weisheit

Aphorismen eines westlichen Zen-Meisters

128 Seiten, 9,95 €
ISBN 978-3-89767-803-3
Hardcover, Pocket-Format
Schirner Verlag

Zensho W. Kopp
BOOKS IN GERMAN

Die Freiheit des Zen

Das Zen-Buch,
das alle Begrenzungen
sprengt

243 Seiten, 8,95 €
ISBN 978-3-89767-561-2
Taschenbuch
Schirner Verlag

Der große Zen-Weg

Der Weg zur Erleuchtung
mitten im Leben

Unterweisungen eines
westlichen Zen-Meisters

187 Seiten, 7,95 €
ISBN 978-3-89767-408-0
Taschenbuch
Schirner Verlag

ZENSHO W. KOPP
BOOKS IN GERMAN

**Worte
eines Erwachten**

Aphorismen eines
westlichen Zen-Meisters

120 Seiten, 9,95 €
ISBN 978-3-89767-339-7
Hardcover, Pocket-Format
Schirner Verlag

**ZEN und die
Wiedergeburt der
christlichen Mystik**

Ein Wegführer
zum wahren Selbst

280 Seiten, 8,95 €
ISBN 978-3-89767-426-4
Taschenbuch
Schirner Verlag